Ta

A Love Story for Grown-ups

By Alicia Ross Erickson

My sincere thanks go to my editor, Joan Claire Graham, for helping me organize my thoughts and see a pattern to my story. Back 2002, I took an Adult Education class in Oceancide, CA, in which the instructor encouraged two dozen senior citizens from all walks of life to write a page and a half each week. Anna Bledsoe, my dear friend, encouraged me to attend the class with her, and I am grateful for that experience. My emotional support system includes my sons, Joel, Patrick and Daniel, my daughters-in-law, and my grandchildren. I especially want to thank my sister, Marion Ross, who read the first draft and lent encouragement and support to the final book.

Graham Megyeri Books is a micro press specializing in

Minnesota non-fiction. Previous titles include *Minnesota Memories* (7 volumes)

Albert Lea Remembers, Austin Remembers, A Boy from C-11,

Poetry in Past and Present Tenses

and *Crackers and Milk.* For more information about *Minnesota Memories,*

see MinnesotaMemories.com.

Take Two: A Love Story for Grown-ups

By Alicia Ross Erickson

Copyright: December 2012

ISBN: 978-0-9791994-3-1   0-9791994-3-3

Graham Megyeri Books

439 Lakeview Blvd., Albert Lea, MN 56007

MinnMemory@aol.com

Preface

I met with Alicia Ross Erickson after she told me she had an extraordinary true story that she wanted to share with an audience outside her immediate family. She had been thinking for the past several years that her experience might inspire readers of all ages who often cling to the misconception that forgiveness is impossible and that true love runs an easy, straight course. After reading her initial manuscript, I began to understand, and as we worked to organize and polish her prose, I came to realize that this quiet, often reserved woman possesses great strength of character and a tremendous sense of adventure,

Readers might draw comparisons to the British television series *As Time Goes By* or to Robert Frost's poem, "The Road Not Taken," or to Sammy Cahn's song, "The Second Time Around" or even to some of Nicholas Sparks' romantic novels, but the truth of this book takes us to a place where fiction, songs and poetry can only suggest.

Take Two: A Love Story for Grown-ups stands as a testament to the power of faith, hope, love and commitment.

Joan Claire Graham
Editor

CHAPTER 1

The Beginning

The early morning sun warmed my back as I sat in a deck chair on the roof garden atop an old three-story, brick hotel in San Pedro. A clear view of the channel leading from the Pacific Ocean into Los Angeles Harbor just three blocks away revealed huge cargo ships silently gliding through to the harbor. Big, boxy carriers brought new autos from Japan or Korea, and sleek, white cruise ships returned travelers from the Mexican Riviera. Here, as I gazed on one of the major harbors of the world, a center of commerce and culture, I savored the wonder of it all. It was my quiet time. This was a plateau in my life, and I was amazed to be here.

This was neither a mountaintop nor a valley of shadows experience like I had known in my youth. No, this was a stopping place, a meditation place from which to look back over sixty-two years of my life, with all its richness and wreckage, and to look into the mists of the unborn future. Could I find and be able to recognize the path the Lord had laid out for me?

In 1978, the old hotel became the port office of Mercy Ships, a global charity operating a growing fleet of hospital ships in developing nations. My first knowledge of this missionary outreach came when a friend at church invited me to see the *MS Anastasis*, which was docked in the Port of San Diego. As we toured the ship, which had been converted from an aging Italian luxury liner to a seagoing hospital, the spirit of the young people who made up the crew and staff stirred something within me. Their integrity and the sincerity of their behavior touched me deeply, and I felt drawn to this atmosphere.

After leaving my fourteen-year secretarial job with the Episcopal Community Services in San Diego, I had spent a year and a half in short-term employment assignments as a Kelly Girl, and I was ready for a change. Friends told me that Mercy Ships needed a secretary desperately. As I began the application process, the possibility of working with this ministry excited me, despite its many challenges. This was voluntary work with no pay. In fact, members of the staff and crew paid a small amount to be involved with this project. It was a labor of love.

When my application was approved, I decided to rent out my San Diego home in order to finance my commitment to Mercy Ships. With my furniture in storage, I moved into the old hotel in April 1987. About forty people, mostly between the ages of 20 and 40, worked, played, ate, lived and worshipped there together. They were highly intelligent, motivated, and dedicated to helping the poor. Several came from other countries: Fiji, Samoa, Tonga, New Zealand, Australia, Brazil, Mauritius, Canada, Holland, South Africa and Kenya. A few of us gray haired people brought wisdom and experience to this wonderfully eclectic group.

The street level of the building housed our administrative offices and dining room. I was assigned to the medical department in the basement, near the computer room, where we kept in touch by modem with the ship and its advance teams. We recruited volunteer doctors, nurses, dentists and other medical specialists to go on short-term outreach missions to places where people had no regular medical care. At that time, a four-month mission in Lazaro Cardenas on the west coast of Mexico was in the planning stage. An advance team of two people had already been there for two years, meeting with government officials, getting to know the people and their customs, and preparing for medical teams to work in the villages and countryside. Meanwhile, we in the port office recruited medical staff, seamen, engineers, and other crew and lined up donations of medical supplies, equipment, food, and fuel for operating the ship. Every week began with a prayer meeting in the dining room. With singing, prayer, fellowship and encouragement, we planned our week's activities.

A full dinner at noon was provided for the staff, but we were on our own for breakfast and dinner, and we each had our own space in the refrigerators. When our full-time cook had to leave, we divided her job up among the women. On weekends, our dining room became a coffee house and drop-in center for the public. Evening snack time in the tiny kitchen provided a good opportunity to talk about whatever was on our minds.

Our little bedrooms were small, but two people could manage if they were considerate of each other. We stood in line for showers and shared the washing machine and dryer. One night we leaned out of our windows or sat on the fire escape to watch the filming of a movie in the street below. Some Friday nights we crowded into a bedroom with a VCR to watch a movie. Occasionally a small group of us went to a rescue mission in Wilmington Harbor to sing and share with people who gathered there for a meal.

All our work had a global orientation. Volunteers regularly flew in from faraway places, and we who had cars often drove to LAX to pick them up. I was sent to greet a nurse from the Island of Mauritius in the Indian Ocean. We had an interesting drive to San Pedro while getting acquainted. Her heritage was African, Chinese and East Indian, and she was a bold, strong and fun-loving young woman. She became my roommate, and we had a great time.

Although our work was serious and challenging, the various funny and inspiring incidents that happened daily kept me in a very positive frame of mind. Of course, with so many young people, there were numerous romances, and at least four weddings.

In this atmosphere of strong love and prayerful support, I began to examine my life and pray for a sense of direction. I thoroughly enjoyed this exciting, enlightening experience, but as time went by, I had to admit that those kids were a lot younger, and I began to lag behind in energy. In February 1988, I sadly relinquished my role in this family. At my final community prayer meeting, Don Stephens, the Founder and CEO of Mercy Ships, just happened to be there. The dear young people gathered around me, and Don laid his hands on my head and prayed that God would help me find the secret desires of my heart. I will always remember those ten months as a high point in my journey. New adventures awaited me. My childhood experiences had prepared me well for my life with Mercy Ships, and my service to this mission provided a springboard for the next part of my life.

CHAPTER 2

The Back Story

I came reluctantly into this world backwards, in breech position, six days before Christmas in 1925. My mother should have guessed I would turn out to be contrary. When she was very pregnant, she went ice skating on the frozen lake alone one evening, fell and knocked herself out. In spite of this rough beginning, I was pretty healthy.

My mother, Ellen Hamilton, was an Irish Canadian who grew up in Tisdale, Saskatchewan, three hundred miles north of the U. S. border. She started teaching school near her home at age 16 and then attended normal school in Regina for her formal certification. While teaching in the tiny rural village of Crane Valley near Moose Jaw, she met my father, Gordon Ross. He had served with the United States Army in France during World War I and was homesteading a section of prairie land in southern Saskatchewan. He was the son of a Scottish immigrant who settled in Webster, South Dakota, practicing his trade as a watchmaker and jeweler while working with his children to set up and operate the first telephone company there. Dad's mother was a pioneer who, as a young girl, had traveled by covered wagon from Chatfield, Minnesota to Webster.

Ellen and Gordon Ross

My mother was beautiful, and Dad, thirteen years her senior, was very handsome. Both were intelligent, spirited and adventurous. Mother possessed refinement and could easily quote Shakespeare and the great poets, things I still remember today, and Dad knew Scottish history and was a spirited outdoorsman. They married in January of 1925 and moved to Minnesota.

Dad learned to be an electrician, and this became his career. He and Mother moved to Waconia, Minnesota, where he managed the local power company for six years. Within the next four years, Alicia, Marion and Gordon Ross were born in the nearest hospital, located in Watertown.

During the Depression years of the 1930s, families had very little financial security, and almost everyone seemed to be poor. We all understood the necessity of sacrifices and frugality. My brother Gordon was born with a deficiency in the bones of one leg, and his medical care became one more concern that my parents struggled with.

During my elementary school years, my family moved to several different towns. Mom and Dad never discussed grown-up stuff in the presence of us kids, so I can only guess the reasons behind all those moves. Maybe small towns needed qualified workers to start up and manage power stations that were cropping up, or perhaps someone needed to educate farmers about the benefits of converting to electrical power. I have no idea how Dad heard about his various job opportunities. Unemployment reached as high as 25% during the Depression, so anybody with a job was happy to have it, even if it involved uprooting the family. I'm only speculating, but Dad's nervous and restless nature might have contributed to his willingness to let go of a relatively new and untested situation in order to grab hold of another, possibly better one.

My mother kept a record of housekeeping expenses from 1928 through mid-1936, in which she documented the dates we moved. In January of 1933, when I was in second grade, we moved to the quaint river town of McGregor, Iowa, where we stayed for two and a half months.

In March of 1933, we moved to West Union, Iowa and stayed until August 1934, when we visited my Ross grandparents in Webster, South Dakota. Then we went to Iowa City, where specialists at the University Hospital made repairs to my brother's leg brace. After that, we drove on a camping trip to my mother's home in Tisdale, Saskatchewan. Our car was a boxy, uncomfortable Pontiac sedan, the roads were gravel, and the trip was long. We returned to West Union in October but, according to Mom's ledger, we had given up our home there and had to live with neighbors. In all the fun and joy of being children, I don't think we Ross kids had any idea of the difficulties our parents were struggling with.

On November 6, 1934, we packed up our belongings and traveled across the Mississippi River to the village of Bloomington, Wisconsin. That place was somewhat noteworthy because it had no railroad near it, but it had lovely wooded hills and fields full of violets in the spring.

On July 3, 1935, we arrived at another prairie crossroads village, Highmore, in the middle of South Dakota. My poor mother was learning some tricks to use in this packing and moving game. She hid a dime in the china barrel and told my sister and me we could have it if we unwrapped all the dishes and found the dime.

We kids watched with some trepidation one day when a scruffy looking stranger knocked on our back door and asked my mother for a sandwich, which she gave him. We called him a tramp, but I think he preferred the term hobo.

Lots of guys like him rode the rails and got off in small towns like Highmore to ask for food and the occasional odd job, and whether they felt frightened or charitable, most people gave them whatever they could.

Marion and I were not very happy in Highmore, and one day, feeling bruised by some discipline (probably deserved), we decided to run away to our grandparents in Webster, more than a hundred miles away. We packed a tiny cardboard suitcase with a sweater and a Bible and started trudging east on the hot, gravel highway. After walking for a long time, with many passing cars showering us with gravel and dust, we thought better of the whole idea. We turned around and headed home, and no one seemed to have missed us.

Dad worked for the power company again and was called out on several stormy nights to climb utility poles and repair lines. I was so afraid for him as I lay in bed watching bursts of lightning followed by cracks and crashes of thunder. But our unhappiness and worry were short lived because in October of 1935, just three months after arriving, we left Highmore and moved in with Grandma and Grandpa Ross in Webster. We kids loved being with our cousins, aunts and uncles and grandparents in their big house. I did not enjoy being the new girl in school again, but by this time I knew I would survive it.

Dad made plans to start his own electrical repair shop, and he chose the town of Willmar, Minnesota, one hundred thirty miles east of Webster. I wish I knew if there was a particular reason for choosing this town because living in Willmar turned out to have a profound effect on me. While we kids and Mother stayed with our grandparents, Dad left Webster in the fall and went ahead to start his venture, and I missed him terribly. Finally, in December 1935, we all moved to Willmar.

CHAPTER 3

Coming Alive in Willmar

Willmar was an important railroad center, about ninety miles west of Minneapolis. The Great Northern Railroad traversed the northern states to the west coast, and its tracks bisected Willmar into north and south sides. Our family moved into the house at 1100 Campbell Avenue. The tracks ran behind the houses across the street, a half block away, but the eerie, lonesome sound of the train whistle and terrible roar of the locomotive made it seem as though trains were running right through my bedroom.

I have an impression of coming alive in Willmar. My memory overflows with incidents, impressions, names, places, and minor details. Maybe it is normal for a 10-year-old girl, on the brink of adolescence, to absorb so much information. Maybe the tense economic times sharpened my senses. I only know that life took on depth, color and feelings as I matured.

With Christmas approaching, we listened to a radio performance of Dickens' *Christmas Carol* with Lionel Barrymore as Scrooge. The weather was bitter cold, and storms had left the streets buried beneath undisturbed, pure white, sparkling waves of snow that were frozen and crusted over. With joy in our hearts, Marion and I walked to school two blocks away, cautiously stepping on the crust and shrieking with laughter when one booted foot broke through, burying us in a snowbank up to the hips.

I was in Miss Clappier's fifth grade classroom at Lafayette School. Each morning we would line up single file outside before marching into the building. We began our day with choral music, where we learned to sing hymns in harmony. The teacher was strict but creative. One time she had us produce our own Major Bowes Amateur Hour. I did a tap dance in my self-taught imitation of Ginger Rogers, and another girl in a ruffled costume did a nicely choreographed routine with bows, curtsies and pirouettes. She obviously had received dancing lessons, but my performance came from the heart!

Like most schools of its time, Lafayette seemed to be serious about discipline. One day the principal came into our class and pointed out a certain boy to the teacher. I don't know what rule he had broken, but he was taken to a storeroom behind the classroom and given a strapping. It made my blood run cold, and although all of us pupils sat frozen in fear while it was happening, no more was ever said about the incident.

I dreaded fire drills because we had to slide down a dark metal chute from the third floor, and we were forced to do it no matter how scared we were. But as terrifying as it was, I never got hurt, and that taught me a lesson.

Gordon, Alicia and Marion Ross

One day Dad went to the drug store to get some Vicks ointment because, like most Minnesota kids, I spent a good part of the winter with a cold. Most of the stores in town were taking part in a contest that offered a 22-inch Shirley Temple doll, complete with golden curls, dimples, and starchy white dress with big red polka dots, as the prize. She was the grand prize, and there were a dozen smaller dolls to be given away. Customers received a key for each ten-cent purchase, and only one key would open a lock on the big doll. The twelve customers who collected the most keys would win smaller dolls. Dad received five keys for his purchase of the Vicks, and I recovered from my cold.

After dinner one evening, Mother finished drinking her tea, and with her sense of drama, she placed her cup upside down on its saucer, turned it three times, and intoned, "Abracadabra! I see many tea leaves and much stormy activity. There are people running around! Aha! I see a doll, a beautiful doll! She has beautiful golden curls and a ribbon in her hair. Alas, now the picture grows dim."

Mother was play-acting with us, but we took it as a prediction anyway. We were not expecting much for Christmas, but it was fun to dream. As Christmas drew closer, however, we received word that we had won the Shirley Temple doll, the first prize! One of our five keys unlocked the box. All those people in town who had quart jars full of keys did not win her. How excited we were! Marion and I felt so blessed, so special, and we wondered if Mother knew something that nobody else did.

A Valentine's Day party in Miss Clappier's room brightened the gray, cold days of February. In noisy confusion we exchanged homemade cards. Looking through the ones I received, I saw one that read, "Be My Valentine! I Love you!" And on the inside a handwritten message read, "I really mean it." It was signed Merlin Erickson. That got my attention so I turned around in my front row seat to search the room for Merlin. I saw him sitting halfway back, a nice looking boy I had not noticed before.

Spring came, and when the snow melted, we played outside. I discovered that Merlin lived two doors from my house on Campbell Avenue. He sat with me on our front steps, and we had long conversations. We sent secret messages to each other with our Little Orphan Annie decoder rings. We sat on the floor in front of our old Philco radio and listened, through crackling static, to Jack Armstrong, Orphan Annie, Tom Mix, and my favorite, Jimmy Allen (the pilot from Kansas City). We walked down to the Skelly Oil filling station to get a Jimmy Allen coloring book of aviation pictures, and we jumped excitedly when biplanes flew low over our street.

Merlin was a slim, lively young fellow who seemed much wiser then I. He was six months older, and to me he seemed strong and protective. As the oldest child in a large family, he saw himself as the leader while his father was away. He contributed to the family income by delivering newspapers and had a confident, street-wise air for a guy his age. These qualities that appealed to me made him appear somewhat threatening to sensible, protective adults like my mother, who felt more comfortable around more typical, child-like 10-year-olds who were not yet ready to even think about boyfriends because they still played with dolls.

We sometimes played ping-pong on the dining room table in my house. Once, when the ball rolled through a doorway and under the bed in my parents' room, Merlin scooted under the bed to find the ball and came up with a ring in his hand.

"Look what I found under the bed," he said. He gave it to Mother. I have a faint recollection of her being irritated and thinking that Merlin had stolen it. This was silly because why would he give it to her if he intended to take it? I have a sense of confusion and mystery about this incident. I could never understand why she was angry, but I was beginning to notice that she didn't like Merlin's attention to me.

We were together almost every day. One time at my house, he was sitting on the arm of the overstuffed chair that I was in, and I became extremely sensitive to his presence. Was he going to touch me? Was he going to sit in the chair with me? I didn't know anything about boys, but I liked this one, and he made me happy.

It was the spring of 1936, a year of ferment. After warning German Jews not to vote in the next election, Hitler marched into Rhineland, breaking the Versailles Treaty and foreshadowing the Holocaust and the Second World War. Bruno Hauptmann was executed for kidnapping the Lindbergh baby. Members of the newly formed United Auto Workers Union moved into position to organize a strike against General Motors. Babe Ruth and Ty Cobb became charter members of the Baseball Hall of Fame. We followed the accomplishments and antics of Dizzy Dean, and a young Yankee named Joe DiMaggio stepped up to the plate for the first time on May 3.

Pan American Airlines began regular passenger flights from San Francisco to Honolulu, and aviation captured the public's fascination. Wiley Post and Will Rogers were lost in an Alaskan plane crash, and we girls always marveled at the record-breaking flights of Amelia Earhart, who dominated newsreels that we watched before the Saturday afternoon movies we loved to attend. Ginger Rogers' gorgeous costumes complemented her every move as she and Fred Astair twirled across the glorious black and white movie screen, and whether she starred in *Poor Little Rich Girl* or *Captain January*, we simply loved Shirley Temple.

Occasionally a Technicolor film would come to town, and that was always a big deal, and sometimes Merlin would protectively walk Marion and me downtown to the movie, through a tunnel under the railroad tracks, and that was a big deal too.

In those movies and on the radio we heard wonderful music that provided the soundtrack to all this coming of age excitement. If you were going to fall in love with music, 1936 was an excellent time to get hooked. George Gershwin's *Porgy and Bess* premiered that year, and who could resist the romantic, jazzy strains of "Summertime?" When Fred sang "The Way You Look Tonight," to Ginger, we imagined what it must be like to have a man look at a woman like that. Whether it was Hoagy Carmichael's "Moonburn," Rogers and Hart's "There's a Small Hotel," or Cole Porter's "You'd Be So Easy to Love," we heard a new, great song every few days. While this music played in the background, we tasted our first slice of Wonder Bread and spent pennies on boxes of "Guess Whats," little pieces of taffy packaged with a surprise toy.

After a few months, it became obvious that Dad's Willmar business would not succeed, and he found a job with the Interstate Power Company. My mother refused to take us children out of school in the middle of the year, so Dad went on ahead to Albert Lea, a packinghouse town just a few miles north of the Iowa border. My father was away most of the time that spring, and Merlin's father, a conductor on the Great Northern Railroad, was often gone for several days. Although both men were lucky to have jobs, we both needed our fathers.

With the end of the school year approaching, Mother began preparations for moving again. I had been happy with school and friends, but gradually it seemed that Merlin was not coming to our house very often. Days went by without talking to him. Something was wrong. Didn't he like me anymore? Did Mother tell him to stay away? A gray cloud hung over me, and I was grieving like a teenager.

The school year ended, and then, on June 29, 1936, we moved almost two hundred miles southeast to Albert Lea, Minnesota. Seven months of rich experiences and blossoming friendships came to an end. Our family would start a new life, but memories of Willmar would always stay with me.

Well, that makes eight different towns in eleven years. Every goodbye involved letting go of friends, familiar routines and outgrown possessions, and every new hello presented everyone in the family a host of challenges. Each child processes the experience of being the new kid in town differently. Marion and Gordon, who must have enjoyed this focus of attention more than I did, went into show business. She became an actress, and he was a radio personality and actor. Since I was the oldest, I had the most experience being an outsider, an orientation so ingrained that it still surfaces in my thoughts and makes me long for a real home. On the positive side, I learned to enjoy change, new beginnings and the freedom to go out and make a fresh start. I do not fear risk because ever since I was a child, I have had confidence that closing one door enables me to open another, and I have faith that everything will turn out for the best.

CHAPTER 4

Our Roots Go Down

President Roosevelt's Rural Electrification Act of 1936 provided federal loans for the establishment of cooperative electric companies. This resulted in construction of power poles and lines to farms and other rural places that had either been going without electrical power or had been relying on wind generators to light their barns and power their wells. By investing in our country's infrastructure, the REA created a variety of jobs, including many more opportunities for electricians. My father's chosen profession finally paid off in Albert Lea, a small city surrounded by farms and villages. For our first week in town, we lived in a tourist camp cabin, precursor to the modern motel. We rented a house at 519 W. Johnson Street, and after a couple of years, my folks were able to buy a house at 508 High Street for $2,000. Later, Dad bought a new Chevrolet, and we were so happy to have a good car.

I progressed through sixth grade, junior and senior high school, and this little city of twelve thousand people proved to be a great place to grow up because it was big enough to offer everything we thought we needed, yet small enough to allow a child quite a bit of freedom. Our house was located three blocks from the public beach on Fountain Lake, where we spent countless summer hours. That same lake became our skating rink during the coldest months and our short cut to school during winter, when kids wore a path in the snow across the ice. I enjoyed social activities like Girl Scouts, church youth group, after school groups and attending weekly movies at the Broadway and Rivoli Theaters with friends. I took piano lessons. In summer, we looked forward to roller-skating in a tent at the fairgrounds, participating in 4th of July celebrations, and attending the Freeborn County Fair. High school and civic bands gave concerts during spring and summer, and one Decoration Day, I performed a recitation of Lincoln's Gettysburg Address at the beautiful art deco band shell that had recently been built by the WPA.

I am the third in line, with my friends at the beach.

On the morning of Armistice Day in 1940, I was set to carry the flag in a parade to honor our First World War veterans. The day started out beautifully, but as young people gathered at the Armory on Clark Street just east of the high school to line up and take their places, a slight drizzle started to fall. I was at the front, holding a large American flag, firmly supported in a leather waistband. Professor Cap Emmons blew his whistle, the music began, and we marched in formation toward Broadway, where we turned south in the direction of the courthouse with loyal crowds cheering us on our way. But as we traversed this three-block span, the wind began to pick up violently, rain turned to driving sleet, and the temperature plunged.

Things got so bad that my flag whipped back and forth, tugging against my belt, pulling itself out of my hands, tearing at my clothes and blinding my eyes. By the time we reached the Hotel Albert, we had to call the whole thing off and take shelter. Eventually we all made it home, where we listened to updates about the ensuing blizzard on KATE radio. Entire books have been written about the death and destruction caused by that notorious November 11 storm.

The school year continued, and I was leading the life of a typical adolescent when I got brave and sent a Valentine to Merlin. Everybody in those days enjoyed receiving mail, so when he replied and sent two small photos of himself, the kind you used to get from a photo booth in the dime store, I was thrilled.

Merlin and I began corresponding, and in early summer of 1941, Merlin came to see me in Albert Lea. As strange as it seems, I somehow convinced my very conservative parents to allow this visit to happen. Passenger train service was pretty good back in those days before everyone had cars, and a conductor's son could ride free, so he may have ridden the train, or he may have hitchhiked part way. He was a very capable and resourceful guy, so it was no surprise that he figured out how to get from Willmar to Albert Lea. Although I don't remember the exact details of his mode of travel, I have vivid memories of that exciting visit.

We had no room in our house for a guest because, like many people those days who were trying to make ends meet, Mom and Dad rented out rooms on the second floor of our house. Gordon slept on the living room couch, our parents had the downstairs bedroom, and Marion and I had our bed and dresser in the basement. We had a tent that we sometimes pitched in the backyard, so since it was summer, our tent became a makeshift guest room, and Merlin didn't seem to mind this arrangement.

He was 16 and I was 15. He came walking up to the back door of our house through the alley carrying a small suitcase, looking very tall and skinny and dressed neatly in a suit. To see him again after five years left me almost speechless with heart thumping excitement. Just think, we had the whole weekend to get re-acquainted! I was bashful, but also proud and overjoyed to have this handsome young man walking me down the street as we went to the beach.

After dinner, I heard Merlin trying to convince Dad that he knew how to drive and could be trusted to drive our car to a movie. He was confident and purposeful, and the drive downtown was less than a mile, so after a long discussion by the garage door, Merlin convinced Dad to let him take his precious car and his precious daughter on her very first date! This was a remarkable demonstration of Merlin's persuasive skills because my dad was very uptight and sometimes irritable. We went to the movie and later drove out into the countryside. At the edge of town we parked in a field overlooking Lake Chapeau, and in the bright light of a full moon, Merlin gave me my first kiss!

Other details of that weekend are lost in the mists of time, but when the time came for Merlin to leave, my dad gave him a ride thirty miles north to Owatonna, and we had a picnic in the park before he either thumbed a ride back to Willmar or boarded a northbound train.

A few months later, on December 7, 1941, the Japanese attacked Pearl Harbor, and the next day President Roosevelt asked Congress to declare war on Japan. All of a sudden, boys who may have been planning to finish high school and enroll in college became men headed to war. On July 4, 1942, Merlin turned 17 years old and enlisted in the U. S. Navy. In order to avoid calling him Junior, his mother had called him by his middle name, Merlin. Now that he was a military man, he preferred to use his first name, Larry.

Later that year, with the country deeply invested in World War II, my father signed up for a Civil Service job with the U. S. Navy at their Panama Canal base, just north of the equator. He contracted to stay there for two years while the rest of us kept the home fires burning in Albert Lea. It was the beginning of financial recovery for my family and the start of a Civil Service career for him.

In those days before the availability of low cost long distance phone service, writing and receiving mail were important activities for soldiers as well as those who were waiting for their safe return. I wish I could explain to young people, who stay in touch via text messages and Skype, how exciting it was to look through the mail and find a letter with your name written on it, anticipate its contents, and finally hold a piece of paper containing words written in ink by someone you care deeply about.

Larry began to write to me from boot camp at the Naval Training Station at Great Lakes. He started to call me Al, the only nickname I ever had. I remember his vivid descriptions of learning to go through a burning building in fire fighting school. In October, he was stationed on the brand new destroyer, *USS Aulick DD 569,* in Philadelphia, but later, until early 1944, his mail came from the Fleet Post Office in San Francisco, meaning that he was serving somewhere in the Pacific.

I was a senior in high school, and like many girls who had waved goodbye to brothers and boyfriends, I eagerly anticipated receiving letters and anxiously went to the library each day to read casualty lists printed in the newspaper. While sitting in French class, I practiced writing my name in different versions of "Mrs. Erickson." One could say I was obsessed with Larry.

On April 1, 1943, I walked home from school for lunch, as usual. In the dining room, I found a letter on top of the big radio. The envelope was addressed to me with a U. S. Navy Official Mail return address. As I picked it up, Marion said, "It's from the Navy—Larry has been killed in action!"

I was stunned, shaking and disbelieving as I started to open the letter.

"April Fools!!!" cried both Marion and my brother Gordon.

"Ooooh!" I groaned through clenched teeth! "I could kill you!" I said in anger. "How could you do that to me? That was not a bit funny!" I felt immense relief wash over me as my heart started beating normally again.

Marion and Gordon seemed to sense immediately that their attempted humor was terribly far out of bounds. They were really too young to understand that a girl in love is not to be teased, but old enough to realize that a soldier killed in action was not something to joke about.

The letter was a V-Mail, a Photostat of Larry's letter reduced in size. It had several rectangular holes where censors had cut out words that could have given a clue about his ship's location, but there was enough information left to tell me that he was in a tropical place and enjoying warm weather. He was all right.

As the end of the year approached, my mother felt disappointed that I would not be able to attend my prom, so she and the wife of the owner of a grocery store near our house did a little matchmaking. They arranged for a nice guy who worked at the store to take me to the prom. I looked glamorous in my homemade lavender taffeta dress and had a nice time, but as anyone might expect, that one date did not derail my affection for Larry.

The weeks went by, and I faithfully wrote and waited for letters and wondered where Larry was. With high school graduation and summer approaching, Mother helped me enroll in business school. Mother was determined that her children would have a better life than some she had seen, and that we would have the necessary education to support ourselves. I don't know if becoming a secretary was my true ambition, but Mother thought it would be a good idea, and I didn't object. Life was good and the future beckoned.

CHAPTER 5

Life in the Big City

Albert Lea felt like my first real home. I lived there seven years, and the rest of the family stayed two more years after I left. I graduated from Albert Lea High School in June of 1943 and enrolled in the Minneapolis Business College in July. Mother had arranged with the college administration for me to work for my room and board in the home of Mr. and Mrs. Wilson in the western suburb of St. Louis Park. I was given a ride downtown in the mornings with Mr. Wilson when he went to work, and the family gave me $3 a month to pay for streetcar tokens.

My room was lovely, the house was beautiful, and I worked hard. After riding the streetcar home in the afternoon, I would scrub the kitchen and bathroom floors one night, iron clothes and linens another night, help fix dinner, wash dishes morning and evening, serve guests at dinner parties, clean house on Saturday, and sometimes take their 6-year-old daughter on the streetcar to her piano lesson. My mind was occupied with Larry and with learning shorthand and typing. Occasionally on Sundays I attended services at Gethsemane Episcopal Church in downtown Minneapolis.

One evening in November of 1943, a phone call came for me. I took the call in the den, and nearly fainted when a voice said, "Hello, Al darling, it's Larry." He was calling from Bremerton Shipyard in Washington, where his destroyer was in dry dock. "I have a few days leave for Thanksgiving. I'm coming in at the Great Northern Depot in Minneapolis on Tuesday evening at 5:30. Can you meet me?"

"Can I! Of course I'll be there! Oh, I can't believe it! I'm so anxious to see you. I love you."

I trembled, cried and laughed as I hung up the phone. It had been over two years since we had seen each other. Mrs. Wilson gave me a big hug and said she was happy for me.

Everyone had an emotional investment in our World War II soldiers and those who kept the home fires burning, but my employer's generosity and understanding of the importance of this visit from my sailor sweetheart was more than any person could hope to expect. "You may borrow my new red wool coat, and you two can have the house to yourselves the night he comes in. We will go to visit friends for the evening," she graciously offered.

Two days later, dressed up in the red coat, gloves, and high heels, I took the streetcar down Hennepin Avenue to the train depot and waited. At last, the gate opened and two tall sailors emerged with huge duffel bags slung over their backs. Wearing their heavy pea coats and navy winter caps perched jauntily on the backs of their heads, they bore the enthusiasm of returning heroes. I recognized Larry instantly, and he swept me up in a big hug and many kisses. He seemed larger than life to me, like a famous movie star.

The other sailor was his buddy Jack, who planned to continue that night on a southbound train to see my friend Betty in Albert Lea. We said goodbye to him, and Larry guided me out of the depot to the curb, where he hailed a cab. When we got to my house, I fixed dinner while he watched and told me how I should cook the peas. It seemed almost unreal. He had come all the way from the South Pacific, we had been together only a little more than half an hour, and here he was sitting in my employer's kitchen while I fell into the natural role of a housewife!

After dinner we danced to records in the basement recreation room. We had so much to talk about, starting with his whereabouts for the past several months. His ship had been in the Pacific, south of Guadalcanal in the Solomon Islands. They were based at Noumea, New Caledonia when their ship struck a coral reef and had to be towed back to Pearl Harbor, which took three weeks. After being in dry dock there for several months, the *Aulick* sailed to Bremerton for further repairs, which gave the men an opportunity to go home on leave.

Larry brought me a carved ivory bracelet from the Fiji Islands and a necklace of cowrie shells from Samoa. Much later in the evening, the Wilsons came home, and he called a cab to take him to his cousin's house to spend the night.

My memory of the actual sequence of events is fuzzy, but our friend Jack tells me that after that first night in Minneapolis, Larry and I traveled by train to Albert Lea. Dad was in Panama, but I recall being in my home with Mother, Marion and Gordon. I remember sitting on Larry's lap and listening to the world premier of Shostakovich's *Symphony Number 8,* a very serious piece that expresses the horrors of war and has been called one of the most dramatic and frightening works of music composed in the 20th Century. Listening to this radio broadcast seemed to be quite important to him. Later we went with Jack and Betty to Fountain Lake Park, lightly covered with snow, and took pictures of ourselves standing on that empty, icy, WPA band shell, and then we drove to a dance at the Terp Ballroom in Austin, twenty miles away. Jack drove Betty's dad's car, but he was such a scary driver that Betty insisted Larry drive us home.

The next day we took the train to Willmar. Larry's large family stood on the station platform to meet us, and there were many hugs and some picture taking. All his relatives fussed over their big brother, the returning hero. We stayed at his family home for several days. On Thanksgiving morning, his mother, Mildred, sent us off to church while she prepared a holiday dinner. I remember the delicious meal at the long table in the kitchen with all the family seated around it.

Family members met him at the train

The Ericksons' older, two-story house was very small for nine people who lived there, so it got even more crowded when two visitors arrived. The family was poor, but the house was filled with love, vitality, mischief and noise. I felt surrounded by their warm support. Images of the home remain with me–the big tin lard can Larry's mother used for a bread box, the kitchen sink with an old-fashioned pump at one side, the cast iron cook stove where he showed me how to make a grilled cheese sandwich, and the tiny lavatory with only a toilet in it. I can still see the large wood-burning heater in the living room and recall how warm and welcoming it felt when we came in from the snow. I can climb again those steep narrow stairs to the bedroom I shared with his two younger sisters.

We kept busy visiting his many relatives in town and the surrounding countryside. We drove across town to his cousin Lila Mae's house, a warm and secure-feeling home. With her mother, Mrs. Peterson, we gathered around the kitchen table to talk. A huge calendar on the wall displayed a photo of a locomotive, The Empire Builder. This great train kept most families in town employed.

One day Larry suggested that I might want to bathe at Lila Mae's place, since there was no bathtub in his family's house. We went there and both had a good chance to get freshened up. As we were coming downstairs to leave, he stopped on the landing, turned to face me, took a golden cross and chain from his neck and fastened it around my neck with a look of love and tenderness that has never been erased from my memory. I gave him my high school class ring. Something in my heart responded, opened up, and I experienced a feeling of sweet joy never before known. This truly was the first time I knew love. We were face-to-face, open and free, but we were bonded in some way. He turned me about to face the oval full-length mirror on the wall of the landing, and we stood there smiling at our reflection as if we were having a portrait taken.

One evening, with the family gathered in the kitchen, Larry squatted in the center with all his little brothers and sisters around him, telling stories about his experiences on the destroyer, *USS Aulick,* in the South Pacific. He told of running aground, about his job as a sonarman listening to the pings of the sonar device and watching the radar screen for enemy submarines. He talked

about the big carriers, the *Lexington* and *Enterprise,* and about the big naval battles. The children, who obviously adored their big brother, sat wide-eyed with awe. These names of ships and places so far away that they had seen in newsreels and read about in newspapers became real as his stories unfolded, and the dreaded truth that he might have to go back there loomed over the occasion.

Someone had a new baby we had to see. We went to a small country church meeting in a school where people sat in a circle and prayed in a simple way. Larry and I sat toward the back of the room and winked at each other as if we thought we were more sophisticated than these folks. Such youthful arrogance! We attended church at St. Luke's Episcopal, where Larry had been an acolyte, and where he and his brothers and sisters had grown up.

We shared such simple, ordinary little events, no different from what thousands of other sweethearts have known through thousands of years of human existence. Yet these precious memories have stayed clear in my mind's vision, to be opened up like little boxes of jewels, to be relived and enjoyed so many times over all these many years.

We must have taken the train back to Albert Lea at the end of Larry's leave because I have a memory of Betty and me at the Rock Island Depot in Albert Lea, saying goodbye to Larry and Jack as they boarded the northbound train to Minneapolis in the cold, dark, pre-dawn hours. When the train pulled away, Betty and I called a cab. Each of us was silently reflecting on the emptiness we now felt and the dangers our men would soon be facing in the ocean half a world away. Would we ever see them again? The cab driver took Betty home first and then drove me to High Street, where I caught a few hours of fitful sleep before boarding the train to return to my life of school and housework.

CHAPTER 6

Back to the War

He went on the train back to Bremerton, and I went back to classes, living with and working for the Wilsons, eating lunch with girlfriends at the Forum Cafeteria or at Walgreen's, and always, writing and waiting and watching for mail.

One night I dreamt that Larry was kissing me. I thought he was right there, but when I awakened with a jolt, I found myself in a cold sweat, alone in the dark, trembling and frightened. What was this? A few weeks later, I received mail from the *Aulick* yeoman, James C. Brown, enclosing a letter from Larry that was written in two parts. The first part, dated January 11, began with a homesick reminiscence about green grass, trees, flowers, and birds and how he missed them. After a break in the words, the letter resumed on February 24 with his account of waking up in sickbay. He didn't know what had happened. Yeoman Brown's cover letter stated that Larry had been taken to the Naval Hospital at Pearl Harbor. Looking at the dates led me to believe that my dream had occurred at the time of Larry's injury. There was nothing I could do but wait for more letters.

Some time later, while I was hanging wet laundry on a line in the basement, the head of the household, Mr. Wilson, came by and playfully ran his fingers up my spine. I knew this inappropriate gesture would lead to nothing good so I made plans to leave immediately. I packed my bags, hopped on the streetcar, and moved in with my Albert Lea friends who lived at a business girls' club in downtown

Minneapolis. They lived in one room, and I shared a single bed with one of them, which was absolutely against the rules of the house. Waiting lists to get into a room were long, but since I was physically there and not about to return to my previous situation, I stayed. Rooms were almost impossible to find anywhere in the city, and my name had been on other waiting lists for a long time. Finally, the management found a single room for me.

I finished business school without receiving a diploma because I couldn't pass the typing test. After weeks of trying, all day long, I gave up. The school placement officers found me a job at Johnson Nut Company on Washington Avenue for $80 a month, but that only lasted two weeks because the previous secretary returned from military duty and reclaimed her job. My next job was with National Insurance Underwriters, who provided fire insurance coverage for retail grocers. Their office was located on the seventh floor of the thirty-two-story Foshay Tower, the tallest building in Minnesota.

When I rushed back to the club for lunch one day in March, I received a phone call from Larry saying he was coming home on medical leave for a few days. He was in the Naval Hospital in Santa Cruz, California. Either he didn't explain or I didn't fully understand or inquire too deeply about the nature of the injury or illness that required his hospitalization. In those days, we all knew people who had received news of dead or missing loved ones so I was relieved to hear his voice, which sounded strong and optimistic. Larry's impending visit proved he was one of the lucky ones on the road to recovery. He was alive and sounded healthy, all his limbs were intact, he wanted to see me, and I was thrilled he was coming home.

This time he came to the girls' club to pick me up, and with suitcases in hand, we rode the streetcar to visit his cousin Lila Mae, who now lived in the big city. We stayed in Minneapolis a couple of days, just visiting and going to see other relatives around town. We played poker in the evening, and when I won a hand, Larry bounced out of his chair and ran around the table to kiss me. He had not lost all of his exuberance.

We traveled to Willmar to visit his family. Looking back, I can see that he showed signs of having been sick. He swore impatiently at his two youngest siblings, and they cried. I took him aside and told him he had frightened them, and they were startled because they loved him so much. I lectured him—so out of character for me! He listened with no comment or reaction and seemingly without comprehension. This was the first time I had seen him respond with anything other than a sweet disposition. Another thing that seemed out of character was that he had bought a pint of liquor, and his use of alcohol was something new to me. He did not seem as energetic or cheerful as he had the year before, but this did not raise alarm at the time because many family members of servicemen talked about how their young soldiers and sailors had lost their youthful innocence because of what they experienced in the war.

Of course, the time came when we had to go back to the city. The train departed Willmar in the middle of the night. I slept only a little, and then dressed quietly in the dark and cold so as not to waken his sisters, Ruie and Nairnne. Larry phoned for a cab to take us to the depot. On the train he slept with his head in my lap—he liked to do that.

Home on leave, 1944

We arrived in Minneapolis by early dawn and found an all-night café on Hennepin Avenue, where we ate breakfast. We sat gazing at each other, just looking across the table with all the sadness of our upcoming separation heavy on our hearts. So many sad good-byes! Could we possibly put an end to that?

I went back to work, and he returned to the California Hotel in San Jose, which the Navy was using as a convalescent facility. On May 17, 1944, he received a medical discharge with a diagnosis of "anxiety neurosis," a very commonly used phrase at that time. The VA helped him find employment, and he began working as a trainee for a title insurance company in California.

By this time, I was living with three other girls from the club in an apartment at Ridgewood and Lyndale Avenue. We four working girls had searched the city for weeks to find this place and, freed from curfew and rules that governed life at the club, we were now at liberty to come and go as we pleased. Larry and I made plans for a fall wedding in California, and he arranged for the church and minister. Friends he worked with agreed to be our best man and matron of honor, and he wrote that he was buying a diamond ring for me. Although we talked on the phone about the cost of living in California versus Minnesota, we never did resolve that question.

In October of 1944, the girls in my office gave me a lingerie shower in honor of my upcoming wedding, and Larry sent $80 to buy my train ticket to San Jose. Despite wartime rationing of cotton goods, I had managed to buy one fine percale sheet. I was given a bath towel, and in my spare time, I had embroidered a small tablecloth and napkin set. Despite the meagerness of my trousseau, I was in a high state of anticipation because my wedding day was only two weeks away!

Chapter 7

A Change of Direction

On a cloudy, bleak Friday, just a few days before my scheduled departure to California for my wedding, Mother and Marion came from Albert Lea on the train to visit me. Saturday morning mail brought a letter from Larry, and I sat at my small desk by the living room window to read it.

> *Dear Al,* (not "dearest" or "darling" as usual)
>
> *This is the hardest letter I've ever written. I've started this over and over again, tearing it up and throwing it in the wastebasket. My tears are all over the paper, and I have to start again.*
>
> *Please do not come to California. I will not marry you. I am going to marry a woman named Betty Jo C., who is to be the mother of my child.*
>
> *I will never forget you.*
>
> *Larry*

I laid the letter down and looked through tears that were blurring my vision at the street below–the gray street with gray buildings, hard gray lawns, gray tree trunks, leafless and lifeless, and overhead, a gray sky. My world had died.

I handed the letter to Mother, who immediately went into protective mode and reacted with anger and scorn. "How dare he be so conceited as to think you would be upset over losing him? The nerve of him!" Her little girl was hurt, and Mother wanted to fight back.

She then told me that Larry had called her a couple of days previously and asked her to travel to Minneapolis to be with me when I got the letter. He did not want me to be alone when I read it. She was very upset with him, but she came. I wondered if my friends who worked at the telephone company in Albert Lea had listened in on that conversation, as they so often did.

I felt disoriented, dizzy and at a complete loss for words. Devastated, stunned, hurt, incredulous, with a tinge of self-righteous indignation, I cried. After I was all cried out, I lay down on my bed and dozed off briefly. When I woke up, I thought I must have had a bad dream, but slowly realized that my situation was true. Listening to the quiet voices of my mother and sister in the next room, I wondered, "How can they be talking about ordinary silly things? Don't they know my heart is broken, my love is gone?"

As the day progressed and I cried some more, Mother and Marion thought it would be a good idea to go to a movie and get my mind off myself. Of course, the movie was a love story so I cried some more. I was grateful to my sister and mother for making the trip to be with me. Even though no one could have seen into my heart, they were the ones who knew and loved me best, and their presence gave me security and courage as I tried to grasp the implications of this terrible news. Thank God I was not alone.

Mother and Marion returned home, and on Monday morning I went to work as usual. I told the president of the company what had happened and resigned immediately, but I told no one else because I felt embarrassed and disgraced. I went to the Soo Line Railroad office and exchanged my train ticket destination from San Jose to San Diego, where my grandmother and uncle now lived. I could stay with them until I found a job and a place to live.

Over and over in my mind this question nagged: "Why did he send me $80 for a train ticket to come to marry him if he didn't really love me?" That was a lot of money, and money was all-important to Larry.

Because I couldn't face my friends, I kept the shower gifts, packed all my belongings, and went home to Albert Lea for a few days. I can't recall if anyone tried to talk me out of going to California, but it wouldn't have been any use to try because I was determined to get as far away as possible. I took the train south to Des Moines, changed to the Union Pacific Railroad, and got off the train at Denver because I was so tired. Across the street from the depot was a plain little hotel. I walked over there with my bags and paid for a room so I could sleep a few hours and get cleaned up. That evening, I got back on a train to San Diego, which was full of soldiers and sailors partying and card-playing all night long. A couple of them were more than happy to let me cry on their shoulders and to buy me dinner!

Coming into California through the desert with its strange smell of rain-soaked sage brush mixed with the pungent odor of orange peels from passengers' lunch bags was a new experience for my senses. My excitement grew as we pulled into Union Station in Los Angeles. I had a few hours to wait for the "milk train," so I lay down on a wooden bench in the ladies' lounge and slept while the loud speaker played "Gaiety Parisienne."

I boarded the train for San Diego in the pre-dawn hours and saw the ocean for the first time as we stopped at every small town along the coast. The trip from Minnesota had lasted three days. At the Santa Fe Depot in San Diego, I found dear Uncle Don Ross waiting on the platform for me. I stayed with him and Grandma Ross for two weeks until I found a place of my own.

It was November 4, 1944, and I was not yet 19 years old. Although my heart had been broken, I resolved to go forward. In my mind I made a short list of resolutions:

• There will be no more thinking about Larry, Albert Lea, or Minnesota.

• I will never go back.

• Starting a new life here and closing the door on my old one will be easy.

• Perhaps I should even be thankful to have been spared a difficult marriage.

• I'll get a job because there is plenty to do here.

• I know I can do this. It will be like being the new girl at school again.

CHAPTER 8

Intermezzo

After settling in San Diego, it was necessary to plunge into life again: to get a job, find a place to live on my own, and establish a social life. I did this by taking a Civil Service job with the U.S. Navy, renting a room in a private home in the North Park area, and volunteering at two USO Centers.

To greatly condense the years, let me say I was married in San Diego in 1947 to a different sailor from Boise. We moved to Eugene, where my husband attended the University of Oregon on the G.I. Bill. I gave birth to Joel and Patrick there. In 1955, we moved to San Diego, where my husband worked for the City Planning Department. On October 31, 1957, I gave birth to another son, Daniel. This baby had a difficult entry into life and was profoundly brain damaged and limited in development. Although his presence in our lives brought sadness and frustration, it also brought moments of profound joy and gave everyone in the family insight about human behavior. Like so many mothers of children like Daniel, who never acquired the ability to speak, I knew that there were no tests that could measure his uncanny ability to sense goodness, joy, evil and impending danger. I also learned by trial and error that everything about him improved when we followed a routine and practiced patience and kindness.

Our marriage had insurmountable problems, however, and after twenty-three years, I divorced my husband, something that was extremely difficult for all of us. Being single again opened up a new life for me, beginning in 1971 with a job as secretary to the executive director of Episcopal Community Services, the social action arm of the Episcopal Diocese of San Diego. This was a challenging job that expanded my outlook on just about everything.

It was an exciting and liberating time. I became very involved with church activities, especially the renewal movement that began in the 1970s. I began to think about my unfulfilled childhood dreams, and acting on one of those dreams in August of 1978, I began taking flying lessons. Less than two years later, on May 13, 1980, I received my private pilot's license, proving that a woman in her 50s can master a new skill.

In September 1985, after fourteen years with ECS, it was time for me to move on to another job. I spent a couple of years working as a Kelly Girl, doing temporary clerical work all over San Diego and North County. These assignments provided more challenging experiences and growth opportunities. One job with a developer/construction company became a permanent position, and I stayed a little over a year, but I began to feel boxed in. Although the job was secure, I felt my freedom and independence slipping away. More than that, I seemed to be squeezing into a mold that was not made for me.

At that point, my friend Joan introduced me to Mercy Ships and made sure we took a tour of the *MS Anastasis,* in San Diego. That experience led to my resignation from the construction company and application to join Mercy Ships. I was privileged to work and live with them in that stimulating and rewarding community for nine months at their port office in San Pedro before I said goodbye to those good friends and moved on with my life.

On February 5, 1988, as I fought Friday afternoon traffic on southbound Highway 405 in San Diego County, I had plenty of time to reflect on the six decades of my life, so filled with interesting people, places, adventures, love and disappointment. I mused, "Despite all the time and energy devoted to those years of growing, here I am with another blank page, a clean sheet to start filling with another story. It's not like starting from scratch because I have my house, my sons, my skills and resume, and Social Security income, which I started to withdraw early."

My immediate plan was to go to Cardiff-by-the-Sea, to stay at my sister Marion's house until the end of the school year, when the tenants would move out of my San Diego house. As I drove I convinced myself, "I'll find things to do. I'll go to the beach. I'll call some old friends."

But as wonderful as all these activities sounded, they lacked the kind of substance I craved, and collectively they seemed temporary, more like a plateau than a destination.

CHAPTER 9

Welcome Home to Chaos!

After my dad returned from Panama in 1944, he and Mom sold their Albert Lea house, auctioned off their furniture, and moved to San Diego, where my father continued his Civil Service tenure by getting a job with the Navy. Mom worked to get her teaching certification up to date so she could return to the career she had set aside in Saskatchewan before she married Dad. She found a position at a school in Rancho Santa Fe, and rather than commute twenty-five miles each way to their place in San Diego, she bought a little house in Cardiff-by-the-Sea, which turned out to be a stroke of genius. Her teaching job lasted twenty-three years, the neighborhood went from desirable to very desirable, and my sister inherited the house after Dad and Mother died. Marion graciously let me stay there, and I found living in Cardiff in North County to be very pleasant.

While waiting to return to my own house in San Diego, I immersed myself in Cardiff life. I learned much by attending city council meetings and planning department hearings, going to the library, and enjoying the beach. Not a bad life, but five months of that was enough. At the end of June, when the school year ended, I finally convinced my reluctant tenants to move out of my house, and soon I discovered the reason for their reluctance.

I found out that this family now had seven children. The father had no steady job, and they were going downhill fast. I learned later that Catholic Community Services gave them shelter. They also helped take care of the children, gave the parents guidance to bring their lives under control, and helped the father find work. I felt somewhat guilty about putting a family out of their home, but ultimately felt glad that they received much-needed help from an experienced social agency.

The list of damages to my house could fill another book! All the carpets were ruined, and cupboards and walls had holes in strange places. The freezer was full of water, rot and mold, and everything needed painting. Well, enough said! I spent the next two months running around buying carpet, hiring handymen and painters. A moving company brought my furnishings out of storage, and thus began another story of lost furniture. But although all of this was upsetting, I rationalized that this was the price I paid for having had such a great experience with Mercy Ships.

CHAPTER 10

A Friend in Need

In August of that year, my friend Joan became sick and was not able to work. She was alone, divorced and too sick to live with her children and grandchildren. Two other friends from church and I decided to take care of her. We first needed to empty her apartment and store her furnishings so she could move in with one of the women. That arrangement was only temporary, and it soon became obvious that I was the only one who had the space, freedom, energy and time to care for Joan. By that time my house was repaired, clean and ready.

So Joan moved in with me. She was terminally ill with heart disease and kidney failure that required dialysis treatments three times a week. The people from our church set up a schedule to help take her to the clinic, and it was a profound and touching experience as the church community became involved with her care. Many people came to visit, to bring food and to pray, and their caring involvement was a blessing for Joan as well as for themselves.

The disease was gaining momentum, and Joan's physical condition continued to decline. Through late summer and fall, I occasionally had to take her to the hospital for a couple of days to be stabilized. I was always glad to bring her home again because she was a dear friend and we enjoyed being together. I was working part-time temporary jobs, and through county social agencies, I was able to receive some financial assistance for her care. As I took care of her, the busy routines of the world seemed less important, and making her precious few days enjoyable was the most important thing on my agenda. As her condition deteriorated before my eyes, I was able to observe how short life is, how quickly our days run out, and how little time there is to resolve old hurts, to give, and receive forgiveness.

The experiences of our youth, when each new adventure takes on heightened intensity, often remain vivid, even as we age. Despite my early resolve to forget about him, Larry had been on my mind for many years, and his abrupt departure from my life more than forty years earlier felt like unfinished business. I thought of all my hurt and about many unanswered questions that I still carried with me after all those years. A strong feeling was pulling me so powerfully that I believed I should try to make contact with Larry. If I did not, he could die, and I would never have a chance to know what had happened to him.

With Internet access, someone today can anonymously find a former acquaintance in a matter of seconds, but in 1988, we had to rely on old-fashioned research that involved calling people on the phone and asking direct questions. As December ticked on toward Christmas, I vacillated between wanting to find him and scolding myself for acting like a dramatic teenager. I would start to dial Information in cities where I thought he might be living and end up shaking off the silly idea. But my urge to find him proved to be stronger than my reticence, and after many days, I took the leap and started calling.

After some initial frustration, I tried to contact his cousin, Lila Mae. I knew her married name, and through a mutual acquaintance, I had heard that she moved to Boise, which by sheer coincidence was a city I knew quite well. I called Information and received a number. Lila Mae's husband answered and told me they had been divorced a long time, but he graciously gave me her new name and phone number. When I tried that, we connected. Although it had been forty-four years since we talked, she was open and friendly. My confidence about the wisdom of talking with someone from his family grew as she told me many things about Larry's life. We spoke for a long time, but she did not say where he was.

The information she gave was helpful but a little disjointed. Considering that I had totally surprised her with my phone call, she did remarkably well to recall as much as she did. After all, she had many cousins to keep track of, and Larry was only one of them.

She told me that he had two daughters and had been married two times. Betty Jo had divorced him when the girls were about 6 and 4 years old, and after that he had spent some time in New Orleans. He had been briefly married again and had lived in Florida. After being diagnosed with schizophrenia, he had lived a short time in a VA hospital, and was currently living in a nursing home somewhere. This information was sketchy, but I got the sense that she really couldn't recall any more. She told me about Larry's brothers and sisters and their families, who all seemed to be doing well. We promised to write to each other with more details. I felt very happy to have finally gotten up the nerve to call her and relieved that she remembered me, accepted my intrusion, and acted so friendly. I was also encouraged that a door had opened.

On December 21, I took Joan to the hospital again. She had not been eating and was having trouble that I could not help her resolve. I thought the hospital staff could find something that she could eat and stabilize her health so that she could return to my home, as she had in the past. I planned to go to my son's house for Christmas.

I left Joan with her son and daughter by her bedside. The nurses had set up intravenous medicine that she could regulate to control her pain. Although she was not talking, her silent communication with her children was very strong, and I left feeling that she was in good hands.

When I returned home Christmas night, a message on my answering machine conveyed the sad news that Joan had died that morning. I really hadn't expected that, but it was inevitable. Nurses and doctors had made her as comfortable as possible, and her family, including two sisters, had been with her. I had hoped that she would recover and be the beautiful lady I had known for many years. But now, mercifully, she was with the Lord, and she would be given a Christian funeral among family and friends at our church. I thanked God for the fun times we had together.

CHAPTER 11

Happy New Year 1989!

Joan was gone, and Christmas and New Year celebrations had given way to the relatively uneventful days of January. I had written a long letter to Larry's cousin in Boise after our phone conversation in December but had received no further word from her, leading me to wonder if I would ever hear from her again. I picked up my old routines again with more church meetings, new Kelly Girl jobs, and even an occasional flight up the coastline in the little Cessna, just for fun. My old energy and enthusiasm were not coming back, and I had a sense of heaviness, which I thought might have been caused by the experience of losing my friend Joan. The feeling persisted so I scheduled an appointment with a counselor friend of mine. We established weekly sessions, and I was very comfortable talking to her.

It didn't take long for my conversations to turn to Larry. Even though my memories were still intact, I had not shared them. In fact, in all the years since 1944, I had only told a couple of people about him. It was good that I now had an opportunity to talk freely about my old love. We continued counseling sessions until mid-March.

I resumed a busy lifestyle, driving all over San Diego to committee meetings, and working as a temp for a development company in Mission Valley in San Diego. In my spare moments, I tried calling the Veterans Administration to find out where Larry was, but they had no record. I ran up against a similar brick wall when I called the VA Hospital in Minneapolis and a VA home in St. Cloud, Minnesota. I had heard from his cousin that he was either in a VA facility or a nursing home.

My annual weekend retreat to St. Mary's Retreat House in Santa Barbara at the end of March was refreshing, and the five-hour drive home was peaceful. Home at last, I eagerly checked my mailbox, and was delighted to find a letter from Lila Mae!

I felt overjoyed as I tore open the envelope and found a picture. Oh, thank you, thank you! It was a photo of the entire Erickson family, the mother and eleven children, taken a year earlier. I recognized Larry's mother, but the last time I had seen his siblings, they had ranged from toddlers to teenagers. As my eyes scanned the images of these very mature adults, my brain tried to match faces with names. The guys looked healthy and robust, and the women looked happy. And finally, there in the middle stood Larry, looking old, gray, stooped, thin and very sad. To see that he actually still existed filled me with wonder and gratitude, and I felt overjoyed to receive this unexpected gift. Reality was breaking through my musty old fantasies! As I studied his face, the deep emotions in my soul, which had lain hidden so long, came bubbling up in a torrent, refusing to be confined any longer. With tears of joy, sobs of compassion, and the thrill of discovering that he was alive, the heaviness I had worn for many months lifted from me. I was filled with a sense of release and great love.

For the next month, there were springs under my feet and wings on my heart! The world appeared to be more beautiful. Colors seemed brighter and music touched me deeply for the first time in so many years. I felt affection for everyone, and others noticed the change.

During this time, my inner spiritual life was becoming more intense. Was I doing the right thing to open doors to my past experiences that had been so humiliating? Although I do not always wear my religion on my sleeve, I have had a strong belief since I was a teenager that the Holy Spirit watches over me and protectively guides my path. I longed for God's guidance at this point in my life and seemed to be receiving it. In a journal entry on April 17, 1989, I wrote, "I awoke from a dream of a hammer about to smash a watch, and I pleaded not to wreck a perfectly good watch. Does this mean that some time frame is about to be obliterated or interval to be erased?"

Lila's letter contained more family news but did not tell me where Larry was living so I wrote back to her. She gave me the addresses of Larry's two sisters, and I wrote to them.

I called Larry's sister, Ruie Helen, on May 29. Although the prospect of finding Larry after all these years energized me, I felt frightened whenever I made one of these calls, and I wrestled with each decision to move forward. But each time I acted, I found great joy. Ruie remembered me right away and said they had recently been looking at pictures from 1943 and wondering what had happened to me. She said both she and her mother had cried for days when Larry didn't marry me, and that her mother had been very angry with him for what he had done. Ruie made me feel accepted and at ease. I made arrangements to fly to Minneapolis, rent a car, and meet Larry's two sisters, and on June 8, 1988, I flew back for a week-long visit.

CHAPTER 12

In Search of the Ericksons

At 5 p.m. on Thursday, June 8, the American Airlines plane set down at the Minneapolis airport. I stepped off to find temperatures in the low 50s with drizzle. I picked up a rental car and settled into a Days Inn, went out for supper, then called Larry's sister Nairnne to arrange our visit.

The next day I drove around the city, visiting the girls' club where I had lived forty-five years previously. I stopped by the location of the old business college, stepped into the lobby of the Foshay Tower, and drove around the beautiful lakes of Minneapolis.

The next day, with some anxiety, I drove ninety miles to Willmar rather slowly and arrived at Nairnne and Don Fanberg's house just after dinner. They had a lovely home with a cozy room for me to stay. Dealing with a brother's jilted girlfriend forty-five years after the fact was new territory for the Fanbergs, and I felt a little strange too, so I really appreciated their cordial welcome. She showed me photos of the Erickson family, gradually getting to pictures of Larry at his worst. They were not pretty, but I wanted to know the truth. His appearance was bizarre, not at all like the guy I remembered. His hair was too big and bushy, and his expression extremely coarse.

Nairnne was a lovely, warm and intelligent person, and we talked a long time. Don was a friendly, pleasant man who made me feel at ease. The next day was Sunday, and we went out to dinner. When we got home, Nairnne played a video of their family reunion. It showed them visiting the old family home, and I recognized it.

The second video showed Larry at the reunion. He looked old and withdrawn, walking with jerky movements caused by a combination of brain damage and many prescription medications. Then they drove me across town to the houses where I had lived for a few months on Campbell Avenue and where they had lived nearby. I wanted to see it all.

Later that night, thunderstorms rumbled and cracked. And I could hear those nearly forgotten train engines switching cars all night, making sleep hard to sustain. Next morning after a lovely breakfast, I drove to visit Ruie and Tom Buckley in Annandale, about forty miles away. They had a house set in the woods, right on the shore of Lake Sylvia. She was warm and friendly, a little crusty but with a big heart. She and Tom took me to lunch in town. Again, we were strangers, but we talked about the days we had in common between 1936 and 1943. She took me for a ride in their speedboat to look for loons. Back at the house, we looked at more photographs. I met their son Bill and Larry's brother Richard and his girlfriend Bea.

Ruie told me a little more about Larry's life in the 1950s and 1960s. She said he could not hear well now and that he could not talk with others because he couldn't understand them. Others could not understand him either because his speech was so poor. They would sometimes write notes to try to communicate when they visited him, but those visits were almost futile because he didn't remember anything or anyone. He had been a serious alcoholic and was taking medication for anxiety and schizophrenia. She painted a grim picture of a very sick man.

I stayed overnight, and just before I left the next day, Ruie told me that Larry was living in the Nicollet Care Center somewhere on Nicollet Avenue in Minneapolis. I asked if it was all right with her if I visited him, and she said she thought it would be okay. Apparently she now trusted me.

I drove on country roads through Mankato, then headed south and east to my hometown, Albert Lea, where I stayed at a motel. A sense of nostalgia swept over me as I drove past the house where I grew up, the downtown where I once shopped and attended movies, and the school where I graduated. But as evening descended, I was full of wonder and anticipation as I thought about actually seeing Larry tomorrow for the first time in forty-five years. Would he know me? I prayed that the Lord would give a scripture to guide me, and when I checked out the Gideon Bible in the motel, I read Isaiah 54, verse 6. "For the Lord hath called thee as a woman forsaken and grieved in spirit, and a wife of youth, when thou wast refused, saith thy God."

I left Albert Lea at 9:30 the next morning and drove to Minneapolis, turning off the freeway at 46th Street. I found the nursing home at 44th and Nicollet and parked in front, went up the steps into the small lobby and asked the girl at the desk if Larry Erickson was there. "Yes," she said, "he's in Room 218–just go up."

Just like that! After so many years–so easy. There would be no warning or preparation for Larry, unless the Holy Spirit had prepared him. I went up in the elevator and walked down the hall to Room 218. I knocked at the half-open door, but he wasn't there. Nairnne's video had prepared me for his appearance and jerky gait, and from the far end of the hall I saw him walking toward me. I walked up to him and called his name, "Larry, do you know who I am?"

He mumbled something in a gruff voice.

"I'm Alicia."

"Alicia Ross?" he questioned, this time clearly.

"Yes, I'm Alicia Ross from Albert Lea."

As we walked towards his room, he said in a loud, deep voice, "I was madly in love with you. You're Alicia Hamilton Ross? We should have married." Then, after a pause, "You've put some meat on you."

All this from the man who supposedly couldn't talk and didn't recognize anyone! In his room he motioned for me to sit in the chair, and he flopped back on his bed, making sure that his shoes rested on old tabloid newspapers to keep the sheets clean. His breathing was a deep, rapid panting as though the walk from the hallway had been a great exertion. I didn't know if this was a breathing disorder or just a nervous mannerism. His speaking was rather loud, as if he had to forcefully expel air to make sounds, and poor muscle tone and poorly fitting dentures muffled his words. He said whatever was on his mind in as few words as possible, cutting through forty-some years and getting right down to business.

"So you're Alicia Ross! I loved you so much. We didn't do much petting, did we? Why didn't we get married?"

I answered vaguely, "I guess it was the war. Maybe I should have been more aggressive and come out to San Jose." I shouldn't have tried to answer this.

He lay on his side and reached for my hand. Mine was cold but soon warmed.

"It's been cold in Minnesota—52 degrees some days." I commented.

"Do you have a coat?" he asked.

"No."

"If circumstances were different, I'd buy you one," he said.

"I know you would," I said.

He asked how I had found him, and I explained that I had contacted Lila Mae and got his sisters' addresses and that Ruie had told me where to find him. I had a feeling that a door was open for me to speak boldly, plainly and quite freely so I said, "I've dreamed about you over the years, about going to Willmar and looking for you. I wanted to come and find out if you are really still alive. I had to tell you that everything is okay and I'm not holding anything against you."

"The day I have dreamed about for so long is happening." Larry replied.

I started to tell him what happened to me after we were separated in 1944. "I took the train to San Diego."

"Shame on you for moving to 'Diego,' " he teased.

I continued telling him that I had worked for the Navy as a secretary, then moved to Boise, Idaho, and after that, to Eugene, Oregon.

"How many children do you have?" he asked. He asked this question several times.

"I have three sons and four grandchildren," I replied.

"I have three daughters," Larry said.

I sat on the edge of the bed so he wouldn't have to turn his head to look at me. He held both my hands and occasionally kissed my hand or squeezed it.

To try to jog his memory I asked, "Do you remember when we were kids on Campbell Avenue? We would sit on my front step and talk about airplanes and Amelia Earhart, and we had coloring books about airplanes. We played ping-pong on the dining table in my house. Do you remember you gave me a Valentine and wrote special words on it? I remember you had a paper route and sometimes yours was the only money coming in..."

"I had two paper routes," Larry broke in.

"You walked downtown with my sister and me to see a movie, protecting us," I went on.

Memories are coming back to me," he said.

"Good ones?" I asked.

"They're of you–they have to be good." Then, "Are you being a good girl?"

I told him I had been married for twenty-three years and divorced eighteen years and had not dated.

I continued reminiscing. "Remember the train rides together when you were home on leave? Remember that time at my house in Albert Lea when we were listening to the premier of Shostakovich's *8ᵗʰ Symphony* on the radio and I was sitting on your lap, which made my mother angry..."

"Your mother didn't like me," Larry interrupted.

"You were aware of that?" I felt a twinge of embarrassment that it had been so obvious.

"Do you remember when you were about 16 and came on the train to see me in Albert Lea?" I asked.

"I slept in a tent."

I laughed, "I didn't remember that! You're right—it was in our back yard."

I studied his hand in mine. It was pale and soft, with well-manicured and perfectly shaped nails. I looked at the stainless steel nametag on his wrist. He said, "Pretty soft hands for a man, aren't they."

"You're not doing much digging in the dirt." A lump rose in my throat and tears started coming.

Larry said, "Let me put my arms around you," as he gave me a big hug and kiss on the neck. "It's so good to have you here. What a pleasant surprise…you got old!"

"So did you," I reminded him. "You have a birthday coming up pretty soon."

"Yes, the 4th of July."

"You'll be 64, right?"

Yes, born in '25."

"And I'm six months younger than you. Sixty-four isn't really very old!"

We talked about his Navy days. His sisters had told me he had been hit on the head by a hatch cover on the ship. He said that was the only armor plate on a destroyer, heavy enough to do some damage.

"And you had to listen to that pinging noise of the sonar detector," I added.

"Yes, it drove me crazy," he said. He mentioned being in a hospital in Honolulu and then in Santa Cruz. Every few minutes he bounced out of bed saying, "Excuse me, I have to go to the bathroom." Or he got up for a drink of water from a thermos on the dresser. "I have to drink a lot of water. It's better than beer. I have a drinking problem."

He was hungry and eager for his lunch so we rode down on the elevator together to the dining room. We sat at a table for four, and he ate everything on his tray very fast while I found a cup of coffee for myself. Other male residents at his table were noisy and crabby. It seemed like everyone else was in a wheelchair.

Back in his room again after lunch, he rested on the bed, and a nurse who brought him a pill talked to him as if he were a child. We went on talking.

I said, "I hear you've been married several times."

"Yes, it's all mixed up."

"What are your children's names?"

"Jill Nairnne and Molly Jo," he answered without hesitation. His sister had told me of another daughter named Georgia, but he didn't mention her. He didn't know how many grandchildren he had.

Conversation was somewhat of a strain for both of us and for awhile we just looked at each other, searching for the old familiar personality.

Larry said, "Oh, I see you haven't changed." He pressed my hand to his face. He was looking tired, and it was about 3 p.m. so I left, saying I needed to get dinner somewhere but would be back for another visit in the evening. I needed some time to absorb all that had happened on this momentous day.

Returning at 7, I waited for him to come up from the dining room, and we went into his room. His memory loss became obvious when we had to go over all the previously answered questions and start from the beginning.

Larry said, "You're still smiling! You're Alicia Ross? You sure were a skinny thing. Are you leaving tomorrow? Can't you stay the night?"

"No"

"Your visit is good for me. I'm waking up."

"Do you want to wake up?" I asked.

"Yes. Maybe you can help me get out of here."

A profound moment came when Larry said, "I wouldn't have known you if we had passed on the street."

"Same here," I replied. "You have had a lot of experiences I don't even know about, and I've had a whole life you don't know about."

"We'll have to get re-acquainted. Maybe I could come to visit you in 'Diego." He seemed more tired, and I started to leave, but he said, "Stay. You just got here."

I told him I would write. He asked for my address, and I said I would come back again.

Larry said, "I won't be here."

"Where will you be?"

"I'll be moved," he answered uncertainly. He had been in so many places that he might have believed this to be true.

I said, "I've gone to so much trouble to find you; I'm not going to lose contact! May I take some pictures of you?"

He got up, combed his hair and sat in the chair, and I snapped some pictures. When an orderly popped into the room, Larry blurted out in agitation, "They took my wallet and pocket secretary!" He would utter this complaint whenever he was stressed or startled, as I would discover many times in the future.

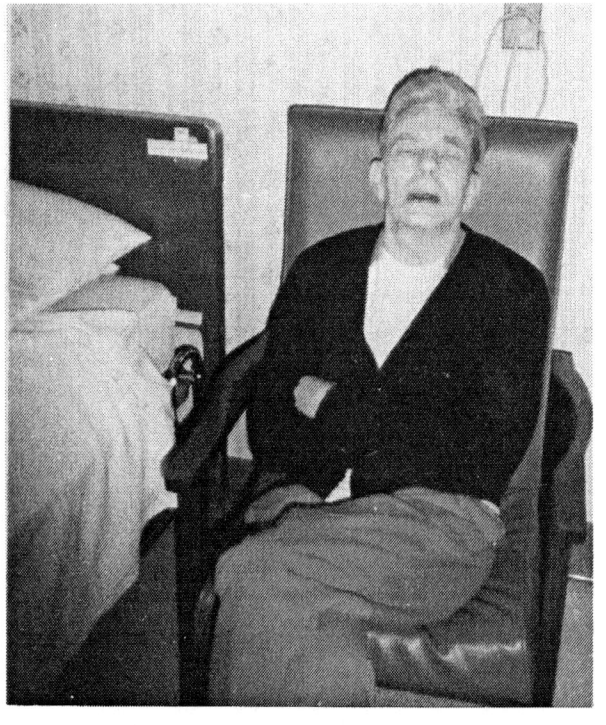

It was time for me to leave, and we walked to the elevator. An elderly lady joined us and fussed at him not to push the button for the first floor. He gave me a sly wink, waited until she got off, pushed the right button and said, "She means well." He walked me to the main door and gave me a big hug and kiss. I walked down the steps to the sidewalk, turned and waved, got into my car and drove away.

Once I got back to the motel, breathless from my long day of unfolding emotions, I called Ruie, his sister. Amazed that we were able to carry on a conversation and that he remembered me, she gasped, "Oh, it gives me goose bumps! It's a miracle!"

Early the next day on the plane leaving Minneapolis, I watched the beautiful landscape fall away as we climbed out. Somewhere down there among the deep green trees and parks scattered with sparkling lakes, Larry would be sitting in the dining room eating his breakfast. Maybe he didn't remember anything about our reunion yesterday, but I remembered every detail, and everything within me cried, "I have to go back. It can't end this way. After all the effort it has taken to find him, now we are being separated again. Oh, Lord, what should I do?"

CHAPTER 13

At a Crossroads

Back in San Diego on June 15, my old busy life resumed its pace. My temporary job with the developer continued. Every day was filled with meetings, work, visits with friends and family. I knew how to keep occupied.

I received a phone call from Larry's sister Ruie on July 4. This was the weekend of their Erickson family reunion at her house, and one of the brothers had brought Larry out to Annandale. He took the phone and gave me a greeting in his gruff, panting voice. "Hi darlin', I love you. When are you coming back?"

"Well, I don't know yet. But I miss you. I hope you are having a happy birthday today."

That was about all the conversation he could handle, but he did sound happy. It was good to hear his voice again. In the following days and weeks, my mind was filled with questions about the future. Should I go back to Minneapolis? Should I look for a regular job in San Diego? Do I just wait? What am I waiting for? I really wanted to go back to Minneapolis. Was that just selfishness? Where did I ever get the idea that if I wanted something, it must be wrong?

My son Pat lived in Temecula, and he was very understanding and supportive during this time of indecision. I began to consider driving back to Minnesota and staying a little longer. Since he didn't want me to drive two thousand miles alone, Pat suggested that his mother-in-law, Ann, could go with me to share driving, so we began to make plans.

I wanted to spend a whole week visiting Larry every day so I could get a better impression of his condition and treatment at the nursing home, meet the staff and learn more about his history. Ann and I decided a road trip, which would take us through deserts, mountains, canyons and prairies you can't see from an airplane, would be fun. She had to be back home in August before school started because she was a volunteer at an elementary school, but that still gave us quite a bit of time.

We started out on July 18, a month after my first trip, waving goodbye to Pat, Karen, and grandsons Everett and Brendan. Our first stop was in Las Vegas in blistering heat over 100 degrees, which propelled us into the Tropicana Hotel for the buffet. We slept at the Motel 6, however. The next day, we drove north to spend the night in Provo, Utah. Unfortunately, my car's air conditioner quit shortly after leaving Las Vegas.

We drove the next day through the beautiful Provo Canyon and on to Laramie, Wyoming, where we enjoyed delicious hamburgers at the Cowboy Grill and Café. The following day's travel on Interstate Highway 80 took us to Omaha. On day number five, we drove from Omaha to Albert Lea, where we planned to stay two days. After checking into a motel, we rested up for a busy day on Sunday.

We had arrived in Albert Lea early in the afternoon so we had time to drive around. We went by my old family home at 508 High Street, where some people were gutting the place for remodeling. We stopped and introduced ourselves, and they let us go through the house. What a disorienting feeling it was to be in my old bedroom again! The upper floor was unchanged, but the old familiar rooms seemed so much smaller. The basement was still the same with shelves along one wall where Mother had put her fruit jars full of peaches. The big gas furnace that kept us warm still

stood in the middle of the room, and I recalled that Marion
and I had used the basement as our bedroom after Mother
rented out the upstairs. In a corner was the toilet my father
had installed.

The new owners were tearing out walls and putting a
partition between the living and dining rooms. A bathroom
had been added to Mom and Dad's small main floor bedroom,
and the kitchen cabinets that Dad had built were gone. We
thanked the new owners for their hospitality and wished
them well. I drove on, and after seeing a "For Sale" sign on
the Johnson Street house where we had also lived, I decided
to call the realtor just out of curiosity. The next day he
showed me the house, which was ugly and disappointing.
But he thought I would like to see another vacant house by
the lake on the other side of town that had once belonged
to our high school band director, Cap Emmons. That house
was quite old and plain, and I was mildly interested.

Ann and I left early the following morning and arrived in
Minneapolis at 10:30. I went to see Larry at the nursing
home while Ann, who did not wish to accompany me,
waited at the KFC restaurant in the next block. I stayed
with him a little less than an hour. Then Ann and I ate
lunch and checked into a motel. After dinner I went back
to see Larry.

Ann loved shopping in big malls so we worked out a plan that
I would drop her off at Southdale in Edina each morning
before driving across town to the nursing home, where I
would stay with Larry until after lunch. That first day, I
found Larry sitting at the end of the hall waiting for lunch.
He still seemed very old and barely in touch with reality. I
sat next to him, and when Marie, a volunteer coordinator,
came by and sat with us, I told her who I was and why I
had come. I started to tear up as deep emotions surfaced. "I
just had to find him before it was too late," I said.

"Do you mean you are still carrying a torch for him after all those years?" Marie asked.

"Yes."

Marie said, "Larry, do you understand what it means to have someone love you that much?" He looked thoughtful and said nothing but nodded with eyes half closed. "He's thinking," she said.

I met other members of the staff and stayed with Larry for lunch in the dining room. I felt very self-conscious among all those residents in wheelchairs and staff members, but also felt absolutely sure that I should be there.

On Thursday and Friday we followed the same routine. After lunch I picked up Ann, and we enjoyed our vacation days by driving around lakes, parks and the Mississippi River before finding a nice place to eat dinner. Each day I would have to reintroduce myself to Larry and repeat much of the conversation from the day before. A soft summer rain fell on Saturday, and I brought him some wild flowers. He seemed more tired but talked about his youth.

Ann and I attended church services on Sunday morning. Afterwards, when I arrived at the care facility, I was surprised to see Larry running down the hall in a clumsy, lumbering gate. He almost shouted, "I'm 64...you're 63... We should get married!"

I stayed only half an hour, and then Ann and I drove west fifty miles to Ruie's house on a lake in Annandale. Larry's other sister Nairnne and her husband were visiting from Willmar, and everybody seemed genuinely glad to see me and to meet Ann. After a great afternoon and evening that included dinner and a pleasant two-hour pontoon ride on Lake Sylvia, we drove back to our Minneapolis hotel.

Monday I got permission to take Larry outside for a walk, hoping that fresh air and sunshine would make him feel better. I was a little concerned to discover that less than half a block was too tiring for him, and this made me wonder about the extent of his disabilities and the circumstances that had led to his current physical and mental state.

Tuesday was my last day before starting my long drive back to California. At the nursing home, Larry was attending worship service in the lounge, holding a large wooden cross on his lap. He sang along with the hymns, and I joined in. Later, I noticed his cotton trousers were too loose on him so I hitched them up with a safety pin.

He didn't talk as much as usual, probably sensing how much he would miss our visits after I left, and I was also experiencing a sense of sadness. As I stayed through lunch and into the afternoon, he relaxed.

"We should get married," he said. "That's a darn good idea. You'd better not say no."

Although I loved him, the reality of what our life together would entail had begun to settle in. "I agree it is a good idea, but it's complicated. Let's just take everything one day at a time," I said as I started to cry.

"We'll have no mess here—no crying here," Larry said in a very loving way, as if to say we could handle any difficulty and there would be no worrying.

We left it at that and said our good byes.

Ann and I then went to a Chinese restaurant for lunch, and I began to feel overwhelmed by a feeling of blood rushing to my head and dizziness. Did MSG in the food cause my physical reaction or was it the emotional roller coaster ride of the past week? As we talked about leaving and discussed how I could possibly keep on seeing Larry, the Chinese waiter came over to our table and said, "It's not hard for you to visit him. People fly back and forth from the coast to Minneapolis all the time!" His eavesdropping and concern caught us off guard, and we broke out laughing.

In the morning we drove south and stopped in Albert Lea briefly, and I called the realtor I had previously talked to. He let us into the Park Avenue house by the lake again, and we took pictures. I thought that it might be a good investment because it had an apartment in back that I could use on short vacations. I didn't yet have a game plan, just a vague thought about future possibilities that were starting to take shape.

As we retraced our route south through Iowa and west to Laramie for another great hamburger, Ann and I were two happy grandmothers. Then the alternator warning light came on, and we limped along to Rock Springs, where a mechanic installed a new alternator and fuel pump.

When darkness fell, we turned south through Provo Canyon and found ourselves trapped in the middle of an Army convoy, going quite slow and making it impossible for us to change lanes. Ann, who was not an experienced nighttime driver, became quite unnerved, but we couldn't figure out a way to switch drivers. That leg of the trip wasn't much fun, but we survived and were lucky to encounter no bigger problems. After two more nightly stops, we arrived back at my son's place on Sunday, August 6. What a wonderful time we had!

CHAPTER 14

Where is Home?

Back home in San Diego I began wondering when and how I could see Larry again, and I couldn't stop thinking about buying the Park Avenue house in Albert Lea. I had taken pictures and could see that it had the potential to become a comfortable home. The price was a fraction of what a California house would cost. It was lakeshore property within walking distance of church, schools and downtown, and only two blocks from the hospital. It also had a walkout apartment in the back, overlooking the shoreline.

After many phone calls and letters from the Albert Lea realtor and talks with my tax adviser, I decided to make an offer on the house. I called a former mayor of Albert Lea who was a family friend and asked his opinion about the value of this 95-year-old property. He gave his opinion, along with names of contractors to call to check out the roof, plumbing, furnace, and foundation that might need repairs. I received reports from most of them that the problem areas were not major.

I withdrew money from savings to make the down payment. It was scary to do these things because I had never bought a house by myself before, but the process moved right along rapidly. I made plans to fly back to sign the escrow and take possession of the house. Can you believe it? That would be my third trip to Minnesota in 1989!

On October 18, I arrived at the Minneapolis airport in the evening, picked up a rental car, and checked into the Motel 6, which was beginning to feel like home. The next day, I went to see Larry. I was nervous after not having seen him since August, wondering if he'd remember me. As I stepped off the elevator, I could see him down the hall putting clothes in laundry hampers. As I walked up to him, he walked on by without showing any sign of recognition. He returned to the waiting room and sat down, puffing breathlessly and looking pale. I sat in the chair next to him and asked if he knew who I was.

"Not sure." Then, after hesitation, he said "Alicia."

We didn't talk much. He smiled when I reminded him of how he used to say, "Grab a wing, chick!" whenever he offered me his arm while we were walking in downtown Minneapolis years ago.

"We should get married."

"When should we do that?"

"When I get out of here."

I had a lot to consider. It appeared that he hadn't improved much, which made the whole situation seem more hopeless to me. But there was a slight change in his appearance. Although the safety pin that I put in his pants in August was still there, he did look a little heavier and healthier.

Many 64-year-olds are robust and energetic as they enter their retirement years, but Larry was the epitome of a neglected and ignored old man. We went into his room, where he pushed the button of a large console TV by the end of his bed. The number 4 lit up on the screen, but there was no picture. He turned it on every day, but the TV was broken and everyone ignored it. The calendar on the wall still showed August. I urged him to tear off August and September because he didn't know what month it was.

I stayed about an hour, and he accompanied me in the elevator to the lower level. With a kiss and hug we said goodbye. I drove straight south ninety miles to Albert Lea and checked into a motel because I could not get into my house until all the papers were signed. I had appointments to meet an insurance agent and later to close escrow.

I spent the next month living in my new house on Park Avenue with no furniture except an end table, an old green patchwork quilt, and a foam chair that folded out to make a bed. A set of plastic dishes and a pot enabled me to cook and eat simple meals. This was back to the basics time for me. Every day I scrubbed, washed cobwebs from windows, dusted, and chased bugs. Several cracked windows had to be repaired. The master bath needed plumbing repairs and new linoleum. I hired a woman to hang wallpaper in the small bedroom. I painted woodwork, bought drapes, had locks replaced and carpets cleaned. I hired a young man to put new drywall in the apartment kitchen downstairs. A roofer came to patch shingles and put on gutters, and I hired old Ben to enclose the upper deck railing to keep neighbor kids from falling through.

It was a busy time and I loved it. Every week I took a ninety-mile drive north to see Larry, who was beginning to know me and was always happy to see me. As days grew short and cold, colorful leaves were falling, blowing everywhere and covering lawns with a crackling orange and brown carpet. Neighbors were burning leaves, and the smoke that hung heavy in the air made the sky turn pink at sundown.

But it was not all work and no play. Every Sunday I went to the church that I had grown up in, where I still knew some long-time members. They remembered my parents and Marion and Gordon, and it felt wonderful to get re-acquainted. Some of my high school friends still lived in town, and we got together for an occasional lunch.

I also spent time exploring all around the town, the surrounding farmlands and villages. It was a step back in time to go inside the post office, built by the WPA in the 1930s. The steps outside were worn and hollowed, but the inside looked shiny and new with its terrazzo floor, brass trim and polished, dark wood paneling. Here was the same place I bought savings stamps to buy war bonds, the same ornate door frames and black marble tables. How lovely of them not to modernize!

It was such a fun time! It occurred to me that there was a dual reason to be in Minnesota. Love for Larry drew me back, and Albert Lea was giving me a feeling of belonging. Both were powerful influences.

As the month drew to an end, my house was ready for rental. I arranged with a local realtor to be my property manager, to find tenants for both the house and the apartment. I was still not quite sure why I had bought the house except that it was such a bargain and seemed like a good idea! On a chilly day in mid-November, I boarded the plane and flew over empty Midwest prairies and Western mountains back to San Diego to wait out the long winter months.

CHAPTER 15

An Unexpected Treat

Back home I continued working at a job I'd been doing since the previous fall, with *Mainstream Magazine* for the handicapped. It was enjoyable work, but I knew it was not permanent. Although I was active, my old life pattern felt less and less satisfying.

One evening before Christmas I dozed off on the sofa and had a dream. I was in a large group of women when a male voice, authoritative but kindly, asked, "How would you handle it if you had to sell this house and move away?" I woke up instantly with a jolt. Somewhere in that scene I had heard the phrase, "These are not your people." The dream was disturbing because I thought, "Not my people? What does that mean? I am not ready to think about selling my house in San Diego! That is not on my agenda!"

After the holidays, in early January, I received a phone call from my sister Marion.

"How would you like an all-expense-paid trip to Minneapolis for a couple of days?"

I nearly exploded with enthusiasm. "Would I! You're a lifesaver! Tell me more!"

"I have a job that just came up. Campbell Soup Company is taping a special show to celebrate the twenty billionth can of tomato soup rolling off their assembly line! Sounds a little silly, but it's a big deal. Della Reese, Robin Leach, Jill Trenary, Rita Moreno, Jack Scalia and other celebrities are going to do it too. We'll be put up at the Whitney Hotel on the river. There's a banquet the first night, we work the next day, and you can go to see Larry! Drive up to my house the night before we leave from LAX. I'm so excited!"

Marion Ross has been an actress since high school, and she enjoyed a successful run for eleven seasons as the mother on the TV series *Happy Days*. She has generously shared many perks with me, which have sometimes involved traveling. After our conversation, I had my overnight bag packed and ready to go in an instant, eager to set out on Minnesota trip number four.

On a Monday morning, we flew to Minneapolis, but the four-hour flight plus a two-hour time difference put our arrival into mid-afternoon. After checking into our hotel, we got ourselves ready for the evening banquet. The group of guests was relatively small, with three tables of eight people, and the conversation sparkled. Marion and Rita Moreno sat at my table opposite each other, and the competition between the two was fascinating. All these talented entertainers and powerful Campbell Soup executives made for a supercharged atmosphere.

Before dinner, Marion had made a call to a school friend, Ken, and his wife who lived nearby. They came over with their son and daughter-in-law to our suite after dinner with china, glassware, fancy napkins, hot Apple Betty made from homegrown apples, ice cream and a big pot of coffee. This was a tradition with them. We ate and laughed on into the night.

Early the next morning, Marion went across the river to the Riverplace Mall for rehearsal, and I went across town to see Larry. He was just finishing breakfast in the lounge outside his room when I arrived, and he was surprised to see me, even though I had called to tell him I was coming. He appeared to be more relaxed, not so restless and jerky.

The nurse said he had been in the hospital on New Year's Eve for observation. The medical staff thought he had a myocardial infarction, but test results had been negative. Doctors were still concerned with his shortness of breath, but they had stabilized his symptoms.

I stayed a couple of hours and then drove back to Riverplace, where the Campbell Soup reception was going on. Guests were served the classic American lunch: tomato soup, grilled cheese sandwiches and potato chips. After taping the show, Marion was interviewed for TV, after which she did a long telephone interview for a live radio show.

After a busy day for both of us, we thanked our hosts for a wonderful weekend, said goodbye and drove the rental car to Albert Lea, arriving in late afternoon. At my new house on Park Avenue, we knocked before using my key to enter. As far as I knew, it had not yet been rented, but a pile of clothes in a bedroom proved otherwise. I quickly showed Marion the whole house, and we left. After checking into a motel, I called the property manager, and he came over with lease papers from the new tenants. In the morning, we went back to my new house and walked out on the frozen lake behind it to take pictures before leaving town.

I drove back to Minneapolis, left Marion at the Southdale Mall to shop, and drove over to see Larry. A notice on the door warned of flu in the building, but after weighing the pros and cons, I decided to take a chance. When I came in, he took my coat and put it on a hanger and hung up my scarf, like the gentleman I once knew. We enjoyed a good visit with many hugs and kisses. He asked again about getting married. He asked how much money I had, which I didn't answer. Although our brief times together had been great and had brought back many old feelings, I had some serious reservations.

He said, "I need to get a job and make some money. I was always good at making money. I was a good salesman because I seized the opportunity."

I said, "Yes, I remember you had a good head for money matters and numbers. Well, we have to pray a lot about the future."

"I agree," he answered.

"Maybe we would fight." I wondered.

"We wouldn't fight—we never did."

Every discussion about spending the next part of our lives together came with an inner dialog between my head and my heart. I still cared deeply about this man, and it was obvious that he felt the same way about me. I believe that there is something special about the connection between people. Some might call it chemistry; I would call it relationship. Logic can't explain it, but opportunity can see it grow to fruition. My presence in his life had awakened him from a stagnancy that had befuddled the medical establishment and rendered him capable of living only a simple, subsistent, almost hopeless life. He felt better now, talked more coherently and looked better than he had before I came back into his life. And I felt better too, with a new energy and sense of purpose, as if I had found whatever it was that had been missing in my life.

But, given what I knew about his past, I asked myself if I would be safe. His sisters told me as much as they knew about his personal life, and I knew that before he came to Nicollet Care Center, he had been in a VA hospital, where doctors had prescribed anti-psychotic drugs and tranquilizers to control his behavior, along with a whole list of medications to control a host of physical problems.

He had been married at least twice and probably three times. One wife died, but the most recent one had notified his family that they needed to take care and be responsible for him. Then she loaded him with tranquilizers and put him on plane from Florida to Minnesota. His younger siblings, who were raising their own families, didn't feel capable or didn't think they could risk taking responsibility for their erratic older brother who had been sent to them because nobody else could deal with him, so they turned to the VA for help. As amazing as it sounds, after I gained more awareness of his physical, social and psychological issues, I still believed that underneath all his problems, he was a good person. But as questions whirled through my brain that particular moment in Minneapolis, I felt the best thing to do was change the subject.

I said, "Weren't we lucky to have these two days together? It was a real surprise. It was so good to be with you again, but I must be going now. Marion and I will fly back to California this afternoon. I will be back, maybe in the spring, but I don't know when. Until that time comes, we'll write to each other."

I left in late afternoon to pick up Marion at the mall and get to the airport for our evening flight back to Los Angeles. As we settled into our seats in the first class section, the movie started with a commercial for Northwest Airlines. Marion started to scream, "That's my son Jim!" Her actor son, Jim Meskimen, appeared in the commercial.

A man across the aisle said, "If you think this is funny, wait till you see the movie."

As the title and director's name appeared on screen, Marion practically shouted, "That's my other son!" We made a big noisy scene and swooped up everyone in the first class compartment into our world. The movie was *Parenthood*,

directed by Ron Howard, her TV son from *Happy Days.*
Watching this delightful film was a treat that made the
time pass quickly.

The flight lasted less than four hours, and I made it back
home to San Diego by nightfall. I had caught a bad cold,
or maybe it was the flu that was going through Larry's
residence, so I slept most of the time during the next three
days. When I woke up, I felt as though life was draining
out of me. It was so cold and empty in my house, and my
thoughts were churning. In spite of the challenges I knew I
would face, I thought, "I must get my act together and not
let love slip out of my life again. I've been given a second
chance, and I must not be afraid to take it."

I couldn't talk much to my family about this because
they didn't really understand. I have to credit their open-
mindedness, however, because they did not make a fuss
the way some people might be inclined to do. Although our
parents had been gone for many years, their values and
influence lived on. Mother talked to her children the same
way she talked to adults, and because of her respect for
others and for us, we grew to be a very accepting family.
My son Patrick seemed to understand my situation best,
and he encouraged me to follow my heart. My resolve to
move forward gained strength, and I figured out a way to
do so without taking too much of an immediate risk. In
the following weeks, I decided to make a trial move to
Minneapolis, live there for six months, get to know Larry
better, and find out if I could adapt to the climate. After
living in California since age 19, I was afraid of Minnesota's
often-brutal winters.

I was able to contact an apartment rental company in
Minneapolis to reserve an apartment two blocks from Lake
Calhoun. I learned that a friend in my San Diego church
had a son and daughter who needed to move out of her home

into a safe place to try their independence. They could live in my furnished house and pay rent for six months, which would enable me to pay for my Minneapolis apartment. It worked out perfectly.

I managed to pack my car with enough household items and clothes for six months, and I planned a relaxed trip starting at the end of March with stops along the way. I first visited my brother, Gordon Ross, in North Hollywood. Then I drove north to Chico, California, for five days with my oldest son Joel and his wife Carrol and their two children. I drove through Feather River country to Reno to stay overnight with my friend Joan's sister Wylma, who wanted to know all I could remember about Joan's last days.

My next stop was in Boise, to visit my mother-in-law, Grace, who was in her 90s. While there I also visited Larry's cousin Lila, who had helped me so much. She showed me old pictures and gave me some so I could make copies. After two more days of serious driving, I arrived at the apartment in Minneapolis, very tired. After dinner I went to see Larry, and he welcomed me with outstretched arms. I was home—sort of!

CHAPTER 16

Idyllic Summer

Spring and summer of 1990 was a very happy time. It was a time of freedom from stress and freedom and leisure to enjoy spending time with Larry, meeting new people, and visiting beautiful places. I enjoyed my apartment, which was small and neat and in a beautiful location.

We worked out a simple schedule so that I could go to the nursing home every morning to stay with Larry, joining him for social activities and lunch. In the afternoon, I would go about town shopping or sightseeing. After the first month, I felt the need to do something more useful so I phoned the Episcopal Community Services to volunteer my time. They happily assigned me to a new program called Family to Family Ties, which matched volunteers with single mothers trying to improve their education and their lives. This was a great match for me because I worked with some wonderful people. I adjusted my schedule so that I spent mornings with Larry and afternoons in St. Paul with people from Family Ties.

I was becoming friends with nurses and residents of the nursing home. They were dear people, and the staff tried hard to make the facility seem homey. Gradually I received permission to take Larry outside for a bit of fresh air, and later they let me take him out for short drives around the city. At first they were afraid he would get violent, but I didn't believe he would. He enjoyed these outings so much. As the administrative staff began to trust me more, they began to ask my opinion about his care. After a few months, they invited me to sit in on his semi-annual staff review, which helped answer many questions. I learned that he had been in a Veterans Administration hospital before entering a halfway house in a Minneapolis suburb in 1978. He wandered away from there so his family decided he should be in a nursing home, where he would be more secure. He came to Nicollet Health Care Center in about 1981. So according to what I was able to gather, he had been living in Minnesota and more or less institutionalized and medicated since he was 53 years old–at least.

At the review I also learned that he had been taking the prescription drug Mellaril to control agitation for many years, at a dosage that was prescribed for people diagnosed with psychosis. I researched this medication and began to worry about its irreversible effects on the nervous system, some of which had already occurred.

As time went on, I asked many questions of the nurses. When the charge nurse's attitude toward me was brusque, another nurse apologized. Eventually it was written in his records that I could have information. I guessed that Larry's sister Ruie had talked to someone on the staff about this change of practice.

One day I stayed late to join Larry for dinner. The nurse came into the dining room and was very solicitous. She said they had taken Larry to the doctor a month earlier because he was eating too fast and almost choking. I thought his problem might have been caused by the fact that he couldn't breathe well through his nose. She said, "If you want to know more, I will set up an appointment for you with the charge nurse tomorrow."

The next day I told a person at the nurses' station that I had an appointment to discuss Larry's medical condition, and everyone there acted as if they'd never heard about it. They asked, "Are you authorized? Are you a social worker? Are you a relative?"

"I'm a friend of the family."

They insisted on written permission from his other sister Judy. This was all proper, but I sensed hostility from the head nurse. Eventually I did receive more cooperation.

Every day Larry asked when we would get married. I focused on the possibility of the healing power of our relationship. Gone were the youthful fantasies that had filled my head and heart about this man in the early 1940s. Although I was not certain I was capable of dealing with all his health issues, I was immersed in the reality of his current condition. Despite the fact that he still struggled with a host of physical and psychological issues, I had seen so much improvement and still loved him so much that, after much prayer and thought, I believed we could possibly share good times together as husband and wife. I began to take action. I told him he needed divorce papers from his previous marriage. He said, "My things are all over the U.S. I don't think Ruie has them."

In September I wrote to the Court House in Ft. Lauderdale, Florida and received a copy of his divorce decree, dated April 18, 1973. This date told me that his physical and mental health had been in dire straits at least five years longer than I had previously calculated. What mattered more than his past, however, were the present and the future, so I moved forward.

I received permission to take Larry out for a weekend so he could attend his family reunion on July 4, his 65th birthday, at his sister's place on the lake. The experience was tiring, but he enjoyed it. In August we attended another family gathering. His 85-year-old mother was there, and they were so thrilled to see each other that the whole family was in awe of their special love.

Back at the nursing home, I noticed Larry's feet were bare and they were bleeding. His toenails had been allowed to grow until they curled under and cut into the ends of his toes. This made me really upset, but he didn't seem to be aware of it. He might have resisted any attempts to groom his feet, or the aides might not have noticed or they might have been a little afraid of him. I decided to fix this problem and took him to my apartment the next day. He bounded up two flights of stairs, taking two steps at a time like a boy, not thinking about his sore feet. He sat down in a chair in the living room, and I brought a basin full of warm soapy water to soak in. Then, very cautiously I trimmed his nails. Such an improvement! We relaxed, had a snack, and I showed him around my little home. As I wished that I could take care of some of his health needs that others didn't have time for, I began to believe I was capable of caring for him.

But Larry was still a sick man, and not everything was smooth sailing. He had good days and bad days. When anxiety was high, he would yell, "The big guy just stole my wallet and pocket secretary! If I catch him, I'll kill the bastard! He took $700!"

I learned there was no point in trying to reason with him during these outbursts. He was in another place, another state of being, and logical discussion would only make him worse. These episodes, which continued all his life, would last only a minute, and the explosive anger was an indicator of how he was feeling inside. There were many days when it did not happen, and eventually it became rare. But I believe he must have been referring to an actual incident years ago that left him angry and scarred.

One rainy day I stayed more than two hours with him. He was calmer than I had ever seen him. Something was different. He just held my hand, eyes closed.

I said, "I thought you were asleep."

"No," he said, "having you beside me is the best thing that ever happened in my life, how could I sleep?"

We talked about marriage again. "Were either of your previous weddings held in a church or performed by a priest or a minister?"

"I don't think so."

"No one from your family was there?" I asked.

"No, they were too far away. We should just get married and forget all the rest of it."

"You mean we should forget all the years in between?"

"Yes."

I was getting ready to leave. He held my hand to his face, and something rose up within me that almost made me cry. I just didn't understand. That feeling was so strong. This was a different day, something special.

Chapter 17

Spring Turns to Autumn

Minnesota's famed theater of seasons passed by delightfully. Spring tulips gave way to big clumps of pink peonies, followed by masses of multicolored irises. Summer was ablaze with bold colors of zinnias and day lilies that glowed in almost everyone's yard. Fields along the highways became forests of tall corn higher than a man's head. Tassels appeared on tops of corn stalks, and maple trees turned to fiery red and orange. Against the brilliant blue sky with feathery white clouds floating in the cooling air, brilliant autumn colors produced an image almost too intense to describe. These last changes told me that my six-month stay was coming to an end.

The lease on my apartment was up at the end of October so I prepared Larry for my leaving and promised to be back in about three months. Time didn't seem to mean anything to him so I didn't think he would be hurt by the separation. It made better sense to take the southern route at this time of year so I loaded up my car and started on my five-day drive through the Southwest to San Diego. The ride provided a lot of time to review all my adventures of the past two years. This solitude in the car also gave me a chance to try to be a little more practical about my future, even though I was not in a practical frame of mind. I was following my heart rather than my head, and I knew it.

By the time I reached Tucumcari, New Mexico, I had decided to take the big step of selling my San Diego house and moving to Minnesota permanently. I would move to

Albert Lea. If the apartment in my house was not vacant when I arrived, I would take another one temporarily. I would be able to visit Larry every week and would have a little more money to live on.

After arriving home in California the first week of November and spending time with my son Pat's family, I listed my house with a realtor friend and started sprucing it up. The young people who had been house sitting left it in good shape so I didn't have much work to do. There was time to enjoy Thanksgiving and Christmas with my family, who helped me with packing and organizing a garage sale. Events moved smoothly, and my house sold on January 23. In the meantime, the tenant in the Albert Lea apartment moved out, leaving it for me. It seemed almost miraculous that in one week I received full payment for my house plus the full payment on a piece of inherited California property that my sister and I had been trying to sell for three years. Now I had enough money to take care of my immediate needs and some for the future. It felt like a confirmation that my life was on the right course, as if the wind were at my back. The moving van arrived on February 16, and I started driving to Minnesota the next day.

A little more than two years had passed since I got up my courage to call Lila Mae, and so many changes had occurred in my life since then. I arrived in Albert Lea on February 22, 1991 in the middle of a winter I had been so afraid of. I drove to Minneapolis the next day to see Larry and got caught in a snowstorm so had to stay in a motel. "Well, I grew up in this cold stuff so I should be able to adapt to it," I thought to encourage myself.

At the nursing home, I found that Larry had been moved to a room on the lower level. His former residence on the second floor had been converted to a locked Alzheimer's unit. One nurse who was convinced that Larry did not belong in that setting had begged the administration to move him down. They finally did, and he now lived in a larger room with two other gentlemen. I was so grateful for that nurse's belief in him. He seemed happier being on the same floor as the dining room and social activities.

The next day I returned to my house on Park Avenue ready to let the movers in with my furniture, and the transition was complete. My weekly drives to Minneapolis began, and a few weeks later, when I walked into the nursing home, someone told me that Larry had been taken to the hospital. They thought it might have been a heart problem, but I found out he had fallen in the hallway and had broken his upper right arm just below the shoulder. I went immediately to the hospital and found him lying shivering on a hard table in the emergency room. He was wearing just a thin T-shirt and a strap binding his broken arm to his chest. Larry had been lying there a long time, and the nurse said it would be another hour before the doctor came to attend to his arm. Sometimes I thought Larry was treated as though he were a non-person, invisible. The doctor finally secured a more substantial sling and sent Larry back with the nursing home's driver. It took six weeks for that arm to heal.

I was quite happy with life in Albert Lea, which was filling up with social activities, and I was still confident that Larry and I would soon marry. While visiting the nursing home in Minneapolis, I talked to a social worker about our plans. She was concerned about my future and looked fearful and talked about Larry's erratic behavior in whispers. She said, "You could get married and still let him live here so you wouldn't have to take care of him."

"No, I said, "What would be the point of marrying then?"

"You could just live together and wouldn't have to be responsible legally for his health or his finances."

"No, we're both 'cradle Episcopalians,' and the way were raised, we couldn't be comfortable with that."

"Well, here's an idea. We think it would be wise for you to take Larry home with you for a five-day stay to see how you would get along together by yourselves," she said. I thought that was quite a brave concession for someone on the staff to make.

"Yes, thank you, we'll do that."

Early in July, I brought him to Albert Lea, and we had a lovely time in the little apartment overlooking the lake. The weather was fine so we could have our meals outdoors and go for walks and drives in the country and not be cooped up inside. We had no problems. The experiment was successful, and we returned him to Nicollet Home.

About a month later, someone called me from the nurses' station, telling me that Larry had been taken to the hospital with chest pains. Although I appreciated being told so quickly, panic crowded in on me, and I was surprised at the powerful feelings of danger I was experiencing. I immediately drove to the Minneapolis hospital. The doctor, who had determined Larry's pains were caused by emphysema, not a heart attack, put Larry on oxygen and prescribed breathing treatments. They regarded it as very serious and kept him six days for observation. I knew right then that I couldn't leave him for long, and that we had to be together.

I found a tiny studio apartment in Minneapolis and leased it until October 31. It had a large living room with a hide-a-bed, dining table, and minimal kitchen appliances on one wall. A closet and bathroom completed this compact space. I would go back and forth, spending four days a week in the city and three in Albert Lea. Under these unusual circumstances, our wedding plans were coming together, and I went to apply for a marriage license.

When he was returned to the nursing home, Larry was still using supplemental oxygen and was being treated very kindly by the nurses. They took me aside and warned me not to cry or show a sad face. We must keep up his spirit. They apparently didn't expect him to last long, but I didn't believe that. His condition improved with oxygen and respiratory treatments.

I talked with our priest, Father Ben Scott, about the wedding, and he told me he would arrange for us to have premarital counseling and would come to Larry's residence for a conference with us later. I planned to go back to California in December and to have the wedding in Minneapolis in February. Larry continued to grow stronger, and his regular doctor assured me he would be well enough. We were coping quite well with various setbacks, but there was one more challenge coming: the Halloween blizzard!

CHAPTER 18

After the Storm, a Dream Fulfilled

Thursday, Halloween, was to be my last night in the Minneapolis apartment. Snow began to fall lightly as I stopped at the deli to buy a quick supper. My car was packed to leave early the next morning for Albert Lea.

A few small children with brave mothers came by my building at nightfall for trick or treats as big snowflakes swirled around their heads. In another hour it became obvious that there would be no more goblins out that night. The radio was warning of a serious blizzard. Soon there was too much snow to even venture out to retrieve anything from my car.

This storm that brought record snowfall to the Midwest originated as a nor'easter, the "perfect storm" that inspired a book and a movie. In Minnesota it brought as much as thirty-seven inches of snow and ice accumulation, millions of dollars in damage and several deaths.

By the morning of Friday November 1, Minneapolis was totally shut down. No transportation was moving, some workers were stuck in their offices, and radio and TV stations provided our only link with the rest of the world. I had a small radio and my Bible and a couple of cans of food plus some Halloween candy and last night's leftovers, but I had to borrow silverware, a plate and cooking pot from the apartment manager. We would be trapped there through Friday, Saturday and Sunday morning as the streets and sidewalks filled up with a deep, pristine blanket of snow.

It was extremely boring to sit in one room looking out the window at snowflakes flying horizontally and furiously. I sat there all day and night with nothing to do but listen to the radio and occasionally go out into the hallway and talk to other frustrated tenants.

By Saturday afternoon I was getting hungry. The wind died down, and some hardy soul walked around the corner of our block to the mom and pop grocery store. I bundled up and walked in the footsteps he made in the deep snow and bought something to eat. To me, this two-block excursion felt like climbing Mt. Everest.

By Sunday morning, the storm was over, and street plowing began. Two men from our building shoveled drifts away from my car doors. As I pulled away, a new tenant was anxiously waiting to take over my vacated apartment. I made my way slowly down slippery Nicollet Avenue and was relieved to discover that I could get through to the Super 8 Motel across the freeway, and that is where I stayed. We had an appointment to meet with Father Ben Scott on Monday afternoon at Larry's place.

We met in the lounge of the nursing home, and Father Scott began interviewing us. Years later he told me that for the first half hour he thought, "This woman is crazy!" But as we talked, he could see that Larry and I had a true relationship and that I knew what I was doing. He agreed to marry us. Thank God!

That settled, I returned to Albert Lea. After a few more weekly visits with Larry, I made ready for the flight to San Diego the first week of December. I would stay with Patrick and Karen and attend to the details of the wedding long distance.

Larry's brother Galen and his wife Darlene offered their beautiful home in Falcon Heights, a northern St. Paul suburb, for the small, simple service, and Darlene agreed to provide food for the reception. I sent a few invitations that included one of my favorite poems, Shakespeare's "Sonnet #116," a 400-year-old verse that sounds like it was written especially for this particular union.

Let me not to the marriage of true minds
Admit impediments. Love is not love
Which alters when it alteration finds,
Or bends with the remover to remove:
O no! It is an ever-fixed mark
That looks on tempests and is never shaken;
It is the star to every wandering bark,
Whose worth's unknown, although his height be taken.
Love's not Time's fool, though rosy lips and cheeks
Within his bending sickle's compass come:
Love alters not with his brief hours and weeks,
But bears it out even to the edge of doom.
If this be error and upon me proved,
I never writ, nor no man ever loved.

Within a few days, friends and family members began to respond and plans started to gain momentum. Marion couldn't come because she was working on the series *Brooklyn Bridge,* but Gordon and Patrick made plans to fly in from California to attend, and some of my new Minnesota friends would be there too.

I returned to Minnesota on February 3, seven days before my February 10 wedding. It was a very busy week. I bought a new bed, arranged for an oxygen supplier, packed Larry's new suit and attended to so many details. The big day, Monday, arrived. With my car filled with two big oxygen tanks, I drove to Minneapolis early. Since the temperature was only about 10 degrees above zero, I picked up Larry at the rear door of the nursing home so he wouldn't have to walk far in the cold. The nurse brought out a huge black plastic bag that contained all Larry's possessions. We said goodbye to his old life and drove first to the hotel where we would stay that night to leave some baggage. It was located only a couple of miles from our next stop, Galen's house, but I got confused on the freeway, and we ended up miles across town. I was a nervous bride, after all. The wedding was to take place at 6:30 so we had to hurry.

As we entered Galen's house, it looked beautiful. Darlene had decorated the buffet table, and flowers adorned the room. Lace curtains gave the place a look of elegance. Rows of folding chairs were set up in the living room, where several friends and family members were already gathering. I had expected that one of his brothers would take charge of Larry and help him get dressed up for the ceremony, but no! They brought in our luggage, guided us into the bedroom, and left us to shift for ourselves. Chuckling to myself, I thought, "Okay, old girl, you can do this yourself. How many brides get to help their groom get dressed for his wedding?"

I assisted him into his new clothes, complete with shiny new shoes that his brother Neal had bought for him, and Larry knotted his tie beautifully. He was a fine, handsome, tall, distinguished gray haired gentleman in his new navy blue suit, and I was so proud of him. He went into the living room to visit with guests while I made myself beautiful.

The wedding was the happiest and sweetest service I have ever known. Father Ben Scott just beamed as he read the marriage service from the prayer book. Larry and I sat in straight chairs, and he, of course, was connected to his oxygen tank. He was serious and attentive and spoke his vows clearly. The words of the service, "Those whom God has joined together let no one put asunder," were rich with meaning for us. Our vows to have and to hold one other in sickness and health were a sobering reminder of our age and condition. We both understood what a miracle it was to have reached this moment of commitment, as the long years of separation seemed to melt away. We seemed to have always been together.

After our traditional kiss, we sat together on the little settee and Larry held my hand tightly. He looked into my eyes with a big smile of victory and said, "Well, we finally did it, kiddo!" It was a moment of triumph.

Alicia and Larry Erickson February 10, 1992

We all gathered around the buffet table and then carried our dinner down to the recreation room and relaxed. We cut the cake and shared this good time with many important people in our lives. Larry's 88-year-old mother, Mildred, smiled as she watched. She seemed to understand that this was a happy day for her son, even though she now had Alzheimer's disease. She did not remember who I was, but she was pleased at what was happening. We were all so glad she could be there.

Most of the evening was spent opening gifts and chatting. It was comfortable and friendly. Finally, it was time for Larry and me to go start our new life. Two of his brothers helped us get into the car; the weather was bitter cold, and we didn't dare to be exposed to it very long. They followed us to the hotel with our gifts and food and helped us get settled. Larry was doing very well and was not anxious or hyperventilating.

Our wedding night was all I ever could have dreamed of. Larry was loving and kind, and we were totally relaxed and happy. All the work of finding each other, waiting and learning to trust was over now, and it was all worth it.

I fully accepted the reality of this storybook romance. This marriage was not the Cinderella story of youth, in which a debonair prince sweeps a clueless maiden off her feet with a promise of living happily ever after. No, this was something more akin to the tale of Rip Van Winkle, in which a character wakes up after many years to discover a new world with new realities and expectations. For Larry, this new world involved a reliably secure and stable routine with someone who had faithfully promised to love and care for him unconditionally for the rest of his life, and for me it meant a life of loving and caring companionship, along with the relentless day to day responsibilities of a caregiver. I have a list of forty medications he took while we were together, and they range from inhalers and pain relievers to anti-psychotic drugs and anti-anxiety medication. I knew it would not be easy, and I accepted that reality. Ours was a love story for grown-ups.

The morning after our wedding, we went back to Galen's house for breakfast. We had to watch the clock. We needed to get on the road back to Albert Lea because Larry's oxygen tank would only last a few more hours. An oxygen concentrator machine waited for him at our house.

With joy in our hearts we set off for home, together, on our own, Mr. and Mrs. Lawrence Merlin Erickson. The joy we felt that day would sustain us until the end of our days together and beyond.

CHAPTER 19

Independent Living

We began our married life in the two-room walkout basement apartment on Park Avenue in Albert Lea, which was much too small. I had been asking the tenants in the upper house to move, but they were dragging their feet on the issue. After a couple of months, the wife's employer suddenly transferred her job to a town fifty miles away, so once more the good Lord had stepped in to help us. We moved into the main house upstairs, which had the advantage of being right on street level with no stairs to climb.

A month after our wedding, Larry was having a bad anxiety attack and I took him to the hospital emergency room. Tests showed that he was breathing well on his own so he was taken off supplemental oxygen, which he did not need again for eight years. What a relief! However, his mental anxiety continued to be an issue.

This was the first time in almost twenty years that Larry had lived outside a care facility or hospital. My journal from June 6 reads: "He still thinks he is at Nicollet Care Center, and every day I have to tell him there is no one else here, no one telling him he can't go out, lie down or go upstairs. Every day he asks whether he eats his meal upstairs or down. I will try more to make him answer his own questions. His mind has been almost totally dormant. Short-term memory is terrible. He still has angry outbursts about his wallet and pocket secretary and carton of cigarettes being stolen. Sometimes I get fed up and tell him it happened years ago and he yells, 'It just happened now!' Today I lost my cool and told him his mind is lying to him."

Larry's brother Neal, a truck driver, was in town for half an hour so we met for lunch. He thought Larry was looking better. I told him about the repetitious story of the stolen wallet containing lots of money that Neal had given him. Neal was surprised to hear that story and told me that he had given Larry a considerable sum thirty years ago.

We were blessed with guests stopping by. John and Alice Ellsworth spent a weekend with us. This is a strange story. I had dated John when he was a young sailor in San Diego in 1945, after parting from Larry. After awhile, John dropped out of sight suddenly. Only his name stayed in my memory, along with a faint recollection of being annoyed with him. But he wrote me a letter of apology that was forwarded to me at my son's house in January 1992, some forty-seven years later, and a couple of weeks before my wedding! What makes it doubly strange is that just days before my first wedding in 1947, he knocked on my door and visited with me and my family after finding out that I was about to be married. In 1992, he went to a great deal of trouble to find me again. We had a few phone conversations, and he said he and his wife would stop in on their way home from the coast in the spring. So here they were, and we had a good visit. They stayed at a motel, and the next morning they joined us at church. They are spirit-filled Christians, and he had recently received the Lord. That explained his need to make peace with me, even though I can't remember what the long-ago offense might have been.

John was interested in Larry's experiences on the destroyer because he had served on one also. He said he could get me some information on Larry's ship. After returning home, he forwarded a packet of *Tin Can Sailors*, newsletters for destroyer men. There was a picture of a man holding a banner reading *USS Aulick, DD569*, Larry's ship. The paper contained a notice of a reunion of the *Aulick* crew. I contacted them, and this marked the beginning of our attendance at four reunions over the years. The friendship of John and Alice was warm and enduring. We had several visits with them in their Florida home.

We were very happy, but independent life was still a big adjustment for Larry. Habits so deeply ingrained from eleven years in the nursing home and shorter stints in various facilities before that were hard to overcome, and the psychiatrist told me it would take ten years to get that out of him. So with the doctor's supervision, we began the long process of weaning him from anti-psychotic drugs and finding just the right tranquilizer. I gradually realized there was a pattern to his behavior. In the mornings he felt irritable and sick, and by 4 p.m. he calmed down and was very pleasant all evening. I learned not to call a doctor in the morning, as it would most likely be a false alarm.

Despite various challenges that we just had to learn to deal with, we had a lovely time. We enjoyed many short trips around Minnesota and Iowa, shopping, picnics, and dining out. Several summers we opened our home to some of the professional actors who came to town to perform in plays at the Minnesota Festival Theater Company in Albert Lea. They were pleasant guests, and they appreciated the free room. One of them was intrigued by Larry and described him as a court jester. He could play the fool, all the while observing others, and finally surprising everyone by interjecting pithy comments and outrageously astute words of truth without hurting anyone.

I held an office in our church so we went to many meetings together. We loved being with people. Larry usually kept quiet, but when dissension started and emotions flared, he would bark out a comment that shattered the nonsense and left everyone laughing. They learned to love him.

We drove to Minneapolis for family gatherings every year and to the July 4th reunions every summer at Annandale. At one gathering, I happened to see a phone number on a piece of paper with the name "Molly Lafley" written on it. I knew this was the name of Larry's daughter he had not seen since she was a small child. I copied the number, and after pondering it for some days, finally called and connected with Molly, who was receptive and cordial. We had good long talks. Eventually she decided to fly from California to Minnesota to meet us. She was outgoing and friendly, and over the years visited and even helped care for Larry when I needed to be somewhere else. We have become good friends, and I am so glad she decided to forget the past and build a future on the biological relationship. Her mother, Betty Jo, whom Larry mentioned in that fateful letter, passed away before I came back on the scene.

Early in our marriage, I started researching Larry's Navy records, hoping to get him a service-connected disability pension. We first worked with the VA representative in Albert Lea. I wrote to every member listed in the *USS Aulick* reunion roster to see if anybody remembered his accident. Many answered but few remembered.

There was one whose name I had jotted in my address book back in 1943. He was Yeoman James C. Brown, the guy who had forwarded letters to me from Larry. He told me the story as he witnessed and reported it at the time. The ship was pitching as they sailed through stormy seas on their way back to Hawaii from the States. They were going through a heavy hatch, and the cover hit Larry on the head and knocked him out. Brown personally transported Larry off the ship in a launch to go to the hospital. He was recovering from that injury when he visited me in March of 1944. We met Brown at a reunion, and I believed his story. However, the VA did not.

We filed this and other information in an appeal to the VA. It took many months to process, but eventually Larry was given a formal hearing at the Fort Snelling VA Center. His brother Neal stayed with us all day for moral support. The appeal was denied and then sent up to the highest levels of the VA for another hearing in New York, where it was denied again, and we didn't pursue it anymore. However, we gathered a lot of information from copies of his ship's logs, Navy medical records and new medical evaluations. Ultimately and unfortunately, the last word from the VA in their transcript of the hearings was that Larry's diagnosis and discharge were caused by "personality disorder and alcoholism." We had done what we could, but accepted their ruling as final.

Moving on from that episode, we continued loving and laughing, watching as the light and temperature of each season transformed the lake outside our bedroom window. Life was good and we were grateful.

Larry got a kick out of his cap that said, "Yes I am a senior citizen; now give me my discount."

CHAPTER 20

God is in the Details

We loved our house on Park Avenue. Historical Society records told me it was built around 1899. Its main floor had a large enclosed front porch, living room with a piano nook, dining room, spacious kitchen with a lake view, and master bedroom with an attached deck overlooking the lake. We had two other bedrooms and a large bath upstairs in addition to a full basement and the small apartment.

The house was sheltered under the leaves of seven ancient oak trees that framed our view of the water behind the house. On summer evenings after supper we would take our dessert to the deck. We talked, chatted with neighbors, and watched the activity on the lake. Young daredevils on jet skis churned the waters in tight circles. Speedboats zoomed by towing water skiers practicing for their weekly summer shows. Proud dads in boats carefully towed their tots sitting in tubes that bounced in the wake. Sluggish pontoons sedately glided by, usually carrying members of the older generation.

We looked across the water to the west and watched the sun dip behind clouds, gradually sending shafts of light to fill the sky, changing from blue to iridescent gold to fiery red before sinking into the treetops. Many evenings I would descend to sit on the dock and swing my bare feet into the cold water. Words from "Evening Prayer" describe the scene so perfectly. "Now as we come to the setting of the sun and our eyes behold the vesper light, we sing your praises, oh God!" It was my time for a short review of the day. As light faded, fireflies began their silent ballet over the sloping green laws. A little more darkness and then the bats came streaming out of trees and roofs from all directions, whizzing past our heads, almost too swift for human eyesight.

It was time for us to go inside and get ready for bed. We were all snuggled in and ready for sleep as total darkness set in. More pontoon boats came out for late night parties. They floated by close to shore, with only their green running lights showing, the soft sounds of laughter and chatter drifting through our open casement window. Curiosity compelled us to sit on the edge of the bed and watch the parade. Finally we gave in to sleep.

Sipping my morning coffee on the deck the next day, I watched a big blue heron standing at the shoreline, motionless on his long stick legs. He stayed almost a half hour, and then disappeared into the fog. Every morning when I came outside, a fish jumped a few feet beyond the end of the dock. He lived in an old sunken tire that my toes had discovered while swimming. Other early morning visitors included a pair of mallard ducks followed by their babies. They floated north in the morning and headed south in the evening to their home in a neighbor's back yard. A long, sleek, black animal slithered along the rocky shore and disappeared under a dock. I was told it was a mink.

We had animal life inside the house, too. In the summer of 1992, our sleep was disturbed by scratching noises at the bedroom door, then across the floor to our bed. The flutter of wings fanned our faces and jolted us to attention. Lights revealed a frightened bat and two equally frightened humans. Larry chased it with a broom, upstairs and down, and drove it outside. This happened a half dozen times, until our exterminator happened to see a large hole in a wall behind a radiator where bats could easily come in. That was easily fixed.

The many squirrels on our property chewed holes under the eaves and roamed at will inside our ceilings. At certain times of the day we would hear tiny feet racing overhead, rolling their collection of acorns like marbles. This upset me greatly, and I hired a man to set traps for the little darlings and take them out to farms. This was a losing proposition, but it was illegal to kill them so we saw no alternative. After relocating eighteen squirrels, the man repaired chinks in the eaves. Well, my friend the red squirrel escaped the campaign that had moved many of his friends and relatives to greener pastures and indignantly sat in the branches of the big pine tree outside my kitchen window chipping and screeching at me. He was furious at being locked out of his house.

Another animal friend was a gray rabbit with a white cottontail that even stayed around during winter. But my favorite was the raccoon that came up to our house at dusk. I would watch him from the upper deck, and he would stare back at me with shiny black eyes framed in a black mask, standing on his hind feet with his front paws together, head cocked to one side. We stared hard at each other as I talked to him.

"You just want me to go into the house and get out of the way so you can come up here and dig in my flower pots. I'm on to you, you rascal." But he didn't scare easily, and I let him have his way with my bulbs.

In this land where nature is both gorgeous and violent, we were blessed with many small wonders. We were wealthy in simple gifts and living in a good place for the healing of bruised souls.

CHAPTER 21

Starting Over

Larry continued to feel more comfortable in his new home. He was more clear-eyed, his speech was more distinct, and his gait more relaxed and normal. In my journal I wrote, "He eats well, gets up at normal times, has meals at appropriate times, and takes long walks. His face is getting tanned, his pot belly has flattened, and he helps me a little by carrying in groceries, and waits on himself in the kitchen more." We bought him a hearing aid for the second ear and new reading glasses. His distance vision was 20/20. A new ID bracelet completed the transition. People noticed his improvement and commented on it.

Because it was important to be around other people, we went on outings almost every day. One weekly destination was the barbershop in the mall. Walking through the doorway, Larry would shout, "Attention! Larry is here!" And every man and boy in the shop would break into a big grin. As the bantering and bragging between Larry and Barry, the Irish barber, got into full swing, I could slip away for a half hour's shopping. Barry was an important part of Larry's care program, and I will always be grateful to him.

Before we were married, I used to wonder if Larry would ever walk away and get lost. One morning after we had exchanged some cross words, I could hear Larry walking around upstairs as I went into the basement to do laundry. Then all was quiet. There was nothing unusual about that, but when I came upstairs, he was nowhere in the house. I was just beginning to feel alarmed when the phone rang. It was one of the nurses at the clinic five blocks away, telling me that Larry was sitting in their waiting room. He had been there for an appointment a couple of weeks earlier and probably recognized the building. I felt relieved to know he was safe, and that he had remembered to wear his coat and hat. I hopped in the car and picked him up, and we didn't bother with explanations. He never walked away again.

Mellaril is a powerful anti-psychotic drug that changes brain chemicals. It is not widely used today, but doctors who had unsuccessfully tried at least two other anti-psychotic drugs in patients diagnosed with schizophrenia used to prescribe it to control anxiety, agitation, insomnia and the effects of alcohol withdrawal. Mellaril warning labels listed a host of side effects that included fatigue, dizziness, twitching and uncontrollable restlessness that can trigger aggressive behavior. With the help of a local psychiatrist, I tried to wean him off this and other medications.

In my journal on September 1, 1992 I wrote, "It has been two weeks since Larry's Mellaril medication was reduced from 100 to 75 mg per day. I can't really tell any difference except he doesn't feel well much of the time. He is making many outbursts about his stolen wallet and is agitated until about mid-afternoon. I don't know if he is getting better or worse. Before we were married, I only saw him three hours a day at most. Was he awful the rest of the time? He does make an effort to appear all right to others. My son Pat, the social worker, says it takes three weeks for the effects of changing medication dosage to show, so I feel I must be patient at least another week before getting concerned. He looks a lot better than he did a couple of years ago, but I don't know if his behavior is any better. Of course, he is on one third the amount of other medications, and that must be part of the behavior problem."

In October of 1992, we made plans to attend our first reunion of the *USS Aulick* crew. We flew to Houston, rented a car, and drove a hundred miles east to Orange,

Texas. Travel was pretty stressful for Larry because it was all so new and it disrupted his routine, but we rested a lot in our hotel room. He enjoyed the camaraderie and stories of the old days at sea. His shipmate, Jack Sampsell and his wife Betty were there from Florida. These were the friends with whom we had shared that long-ago photo shoot at the Albert Lea band shell followed by a trip to the Terp Ballroom in Austin, and it was wonderful to see them after so many years. The other crewmen who attended were so kind and considerate of him. As members of the first crew commissioned with the ship, he and the others received "plank owner" certificates.

When our plane landed back in Minneapolis, Larry's brother and sister met us and told us the sad news that their mother, Mildred Erickson, had died a few days earlier at the age of 89. Not wanting to spoil our vacation, they waited to tell us on our return. They may have been afraid that Larry's reaction to the news might be violent because he had such a deep love for his mother, but he took the news with matter-of-fact calmness.

We stayed overnight with his brother and drove to Willmar for the funeral the next day. Larry was one of the pallbearers, and he carried himself with dignity through the long day. All of Mildred's eleven children were there to honor the mother they loved so much.

By Christmas, Larry's twice-a-day medications had been reduced to 50 mg of Mellaril, plus 200 mg of Theophylline for respiratory problems and Seldane, an antihistamine. A doctor monitored his progress regularly.

I still felt uncomfortable leaving him alone. The nurse and the home health aide both came one day in December so I could go to lunch with six of my high school friends. Then, even though the weather was three degrees below zero, I went shopping for our first Christmas together. It would be a quiet day, and there would be very few gifts, but we had the best gift, the company of one other.

CHAPTER 22

Anecdotes

With the holidays over, we hopped on a plane from Minneapolis to Ft. Myers, Florida. Our friends John and Alice had invited us to stay with them for three weeks in February to escape the cold and to celebrate our first anniversary. We had a great time sightseeing, playing cribbage, visiting the Everglades, seeing the Lipizzaner Stallions and just loafing. We even went to Disney World.

Back home again, we slipped into a dull but comfortable routine, but as soon as the weather warmed up a bit, I started a remodeling project in the basement. The northwest corner of the exterior wall needed to be knocked out and rebuilt because it had holes big enough for snow to blow in. We found just the right man for the job.

He jacked up the floor of the dining room above and started to knock down bricks, remove windows, bulldoze the dirt away and make total wreckage. It would have upset Larry to watch the mess so he stayed upstairs and ignored the whole thing while I marveled that ordinary men could have so much fun creating a new basement.

Larry's emotional condition was always unpredictable. One night I was suddenly awakened from a sound sleep by being kicked quite hard. Larry's arms and legs were thrashing about. I jumped out of bed and turned on a light. He awoke from his nightmare sputtering, "Oh, oh, my darling, I'm so sorry! Oh, honey, I didn't know! I didn't mean to hurt you! I thought I saw a man with a gun standing in the stairwell, and I was going to fight him! Oh, sweetheart, forgive me!"

Of course, I did forgive him for this and for his occasional angry outbursts. Experience with my son Daniel had taught me that the best way to cope with this type of energy surge is to take a deep breath, stay calm and patiently wait for the tempest to pass. I wondered what kind of experiences in his previous life caused Larry to have such fears, but I didn't pry. Those things belonged buried in the mists of the past. These kicking episodes happened occasionally, but I learned to recognize the first signs of restlessness so I could jump out of the way in a flash. These spells diminished as he was weaned from mind-altering drugs, but they began to return as he neared the end of his life.

Our life wasn't all high drama. We did the same things most retired couples do in their leisure time, including some mini-vacations. One was a trip to Overland Park, near Kansas City, where we stayed with Larry's brother Gary and his wife Florence and their two daughters. Marion was acting in a production of *Steel Magnolias* at a dinner theater in Overland Park. The four of us enjoyed a delicious dinner followed by the performance, which was excellent.

After the play, we went to a restaurant with some of the cast and directors for a lively recap of the evening. It was an entirely new experience for Larry, who had never even heard of a dinner theater.

At home our evening dinner was usually special, and we ate at the big table in the dining room. I put in extra leaves, and seated each of us at opposite ends so we had plenty of room. I had observed that Larry would become agitated when others invaded his space so our meals were more pleasant at the bigger table. After dinner he relaxed in the recliner to watch television, and I sat at my desk writing letters. How sweet it was to look up and see him watching me with a serene look of gentleness.

"I was just thinking of how much I love you. How lucky we are!" he said.

Every day I would hear him say, "I love you" many times, with kisses blown my way and kisses on my hands. And I was thinking, "How little it takes to make me happy; he knows how to say it."

CHAPTER 23

Strong Wills Collide

In the last weeks of 1993, we planned to get away from the cold winter and stay a month in Cardiff-by-the-Sea, California. We flew from Minneapolis to San Diego and settled right in. Marion very generously offered her vacation house and her older Cadillac for us to use. We really appreciated the privacy and convenience as well as the savings. It was our home base from which to visit my son in Temecula and take tours of San Diego County that included a drive to the observatory on Palomar Mountain. We enjoyed the small museum with its gorgeous photos of the shining nebulae and galaxies seen through the huge telescope, but Larry couldn't walk up the long hill to the observatory dome.

On another outing, we drove up the I-405 freeway to Marion's house in Woodland Hills, stopping in Laguna Beach at a tiny French café for lunch and walking on the beach. We stayed overnight at her beautiful, spacious house with its swimming pool and tennis court. It was all very grand, and we enjoyed being snowbirds from Minnesota.

Our month of leisure in Cardiff came to an end. As the sun sparkled through the leaded glass window over our bed, we roused ourselves for a busy day of packing and flying home. I tidied up the breakfast dishes (must leave the kitchen spotless) and headed for the next room to clean. I started stripping the bed to wash the sheets, mindful of the minutes swiftly ticking away. Larry came running into the bedroom shouting, "What are you doing? You're not supposed to touch that! Those sheets belong to somebody else! You'll get in trouble–they could put you in jail! Stop!"

He grabbed one end of the sheets that I was trying to take to the washing machine near the kitchen. He pulled and I pulled back. Now we were getting really excited. "Let go of the sheet! I have to wash these so I can make up the bed!"

Larry's anxiety quickly reached the unreasonable stage. "You can't take those sheets! This is not our house!"

We struggled down the hall in a tug-of-war with the sheets. He grabbed my shoulders to stop me. I yelled back, with my Irish blood stirring up ferocious strength, "Larry, this is my sister's house. She is family. I have every right to be here cleaning up this house. Nobody is going to stop us. We have to make up the bed, finish packing, get to the airport to fly to Minneapolis, and we are not going to be late for that! Now give me the sheet and get out of my way!" I gritted my teeth and pinned him to the wall. He hesitated and stared at me with wide eyes while I ran to the washing machine.

I had scared him. God forgive me! But he never tried to use force with me again. I probably learned never to provoke his anxiety to that extent again either. It was a heart-pounding little episode, really pretty funny. This was another time when I was grateful for his short-term memory loss. We made it to the airport in San Diego, and four hours later we landed in Minneapolis, and all was forgotten.

Larry, Marion and Alicia in Woodland Hills

CHAPTER 24

Mixing Past and Present

We seemed to be happiest while traveling in the car. So, in May of 1995, when the long winter was over and spring began reviving us, I decided to visit my first mother-in-law, Grace, in Boise. She was 97 years old, and I felt an urgency to see her once more while her mind was still sound. We had a good relationship, and I felt she would be accepting of Larry also.

I eagerly began making plans for driving to Idaho. I wrote to Grace, to Larry's brother Dick and his wife, and to his cousin Lila, all of them in Boise. I loved the anticipation and planning of every little detail. We reserved motels for four nights on the road, and we planned to be gone for two weeks. Our route would start on Interstate Highway 90 west to Rapid City, South Dakota. We would proceed to Sheridan, Wyoming, Billings and Butte, Montana, turn south to Idaho Falls, and finally west to Boise. The famous cowboy town of Wall, South Dakota would be our first night's resting place.

Before leaving, I wanted to put the redwood picnic table on the deck for our downstairs tenant, Sindi, to use. She and I carried it out of the basement, with Sindi taking the lead and me on the end.

She was a strong girl who vigorously bounded up the two steps to the deck. This shifted the weight to my end. I lost my grip, and the table slipped, falling onto my shin with a hard scraping. Instantly blood flowed down my left leg, and I was in a state of shock. Sindi ran inside for a towel to wrap around my leg, and I held it there while she drove me to the emergency room two blocks away. My mind was spinning with all my carefully made travel plans that had been disrupted like a bag of spilled marbles.

The doctor put in some stitches, bandaged the wound and advised me to keep my leg elevated for several days. Well, that was not in my plans. After dutifully considering that option for a few minutes, I decided we would start on the road the next day as scheduled. We were all packed, relatives and motels were expecting us, and we would go. Although my leg would not be elevated, it would be immobilized all the time I was driving.

Our first day's drive was easy, but when we stopped at night, I was hurting. In the motel I could elevate my leg and put ice on it. My wound was still worrying me, however, so I planned to stop at the hospital in Rapid City, an hour's drive the next morning. In the ER they applied a clean bandage and recommended that I stay in a motel another night to rest. But the doctor did admit that I would survive if we kept on driving. So we did.

We drove through the Big Sky country of Montana, past empty rolling hills still covered with patches of snow, with no sign of human life for many miles. We spent the night in Billings, drove northwest to Butte, then south to Idaho Falls for another night. The next day we arrived in Boise.

My leg was still hurting, but as long as we were busy, I could ignore it. We planned to stay five days in Boise, in a motel by the airport up on the "bench." We spent two hours each day visiting Grace at her lovely little house on the corner. She had lived there since 1948 and now had live-in caregivers. For her to be in a nursing home would have been unthinkable. I found her to be quite changed since my visit in the spring of 1990. She was heavy and bloated, sitting in a wheelchair watching television. With her mind as clear as always, she enjoyed watching *Wheel of Fortune* and playing along. She told me all the news of her big family, as well as the political situation in Boise, the state, and the world. Her views were practical, direct and sensible with the wisdom of many years.

Larry was very kind to her as he always was with the elderly. We all enjoyed our visits, talking about earlier years and looking at pictures of my children and her nieces and nephews. It was the happiest time Grace and I ever had together, making me feel certain that it was right that we had come.

We spent our afternoons and evenings with Larry's family across town, where we enjoyed picnic dinners under a tree at his brother's house. We ate dinner in a nice restaurant with Dick, Bea and Lila. One afternoon we drove up into the mountains north of Boise, to Bogus Basin, a ski resort where I had broken a leg (the same left leg) while learning to ski back in 1947.

I drove around town to show Larry where I had lived in 1946. We went out in the country along the Boise River to see the Lucky Peak Dam. We drove by the Veterans Administration hospital, where I had worked for the Adjudication Department in a temporary Quonset hut after World War II. I marveled at how big and sophisticated Boise had become and how little of it had stayed as it looked in my memory.

We had a happy time visiting for five days before heading our car in a more southerly route on Interstate Highway 80 for an uneventful trip back to Albert Lea. We left feeling assured and happy that our efforts gave us a long, cordial visit with Grace. She passed away the following year, and I thanked God for the example of her good life.

CHAPTER 25

A Peripatetic Couple

"I want a new life!" Larry blurted out unexpectedly. "How long have I been sick? Won't we be glad when my brain starts working?"

Amen to that! I was glad that he could express that heartfelt cry for recovery. It sounded like growth to me, but I knew that achieving that new life would be his uphill struggle. He was sleeping better, and his nightmares stopped. His psychiatrist saw no depression as she dismissed him after an exam with, "I'll see you in a year."

He began pulmonary rehabilitation therapy at the Health Reach gym operated by Mayo Clinic in Albert Lea. It was fun for him to exercise twice a week. His friend Doug came to visit for a couple of hours two days a week, and on Wednesdays a home health aide came to clean house and watch him so I could take a break.

Like many Minnesotans, Larry followed the Vikings and Twins on television, and we both got hooked on a long-running PBS series called *As Time Goes By,* starring Judi Dench and Geoffrey Palmer as a couple who reunite after losing track of one another for thirty-eight years. I guess you could say we could relate to that! Larry would help me clean up the kitchen after dinner, and sometimes I'd play the piano while he listened appreciatively. We watched the news, entertained friends, and went for long walks. Whenever Janet Reno, the first female Attorney General, appeared on *Face the Nation* or CNN, he listened to what she had to say and expressed admiration for her. The fact that he admired people with high ideals and intelligence told me that he had a good, sound core and that he had learned solid values from his mother. He wanted a better quality of life than what he had experienced, and despite his previous failed relationships, he respected and admired women. He had good taste when it came to music, literature, and people. While he was living in the assisted living facility, he must have experienced frustration at being separated from various things he loved.

We took advantage of small town delights that included spaghetti dinners at the American Legion, Sunday breakfast at the VFW, political suppers at the Union Center, the fly-in breakfast at the airport, Cinco de Mayo Mexican dinners at church, and the chili cook-off at the junior college. One of my favorite events was the Rendezvous in October, a reenactment of the days of the fur trappers who explored Minnesota. Folks camped for three days, setting up teepees in a lakeside park, demonstrating their skills to the public, and selling roast pig sandwiches. Always eating!

In June my son Pat took his family to Boise to visit his 98-year-old grandmother Grace. They planned to follow that up with a quick camping trip to the Grand Teton National Park in Wyoming. I thought about him being only a few hundred miles away and then, remembering that we had made the drive to Boise the previous year with no trouble, I decided we would drive to Jackson Hole Lodge in Wyoming. We arranged to meet Pat at their campsite at Jenny Lake. We arrived on a Monday. On Tuesday we looked for them at the camp unsuccessfully, but we thought we knew which tent was theirs so I left them a note. We went back to our place and prepared a nice dinner, and Pat and Karen and the boys eventually knocked on the door of our lodge. Our room had a bed that folded up into the wall so there was a lot of space for a great party. We also had an indoor shower that the campers were happy to use.

They went back to camp for the night, and the next day all six of us toured the countryside. The scenery was spectacular with the jagged Teton Mountains in the background. We all went out to a restaurant for dinner before saying goodbye. We departed the next day and arrived home on Friday. I was so glad we took that trip, but the high altitude had challenged Larry's breathing so I knew we would never go into the mountains again.

Larry liked being active as much as I did, and he used to say, "A dead ocean has no waves." So we made more waves by flying to San Diego for three weeks at Thanksgiving time. We were enjoying this fourth year of our marriage and grateful for reasonably good health.

Larry and Marion at the Itasca Rock Garden in Albert Lea

CHAPTER 26

The Healing Arts

Two topics dominated our lives from 1997 through 2001. One was our service at Christ Episcopal Church, and the other was time spent with the medical profession at the clinic and hospital.

After serving as church treasurer for five years, I graduated to junior warden, then senior warden for three years. It was a challenging time to be senior warden because our young rector resigned in 1998, and the parish went through the process of searching for a new priest, which consumed almost two and a half years. For the first six months, substitute priests served our church. Then we were blessed by having Rev. Jim Jenkins commute from Minneapolis to lead us part time for two years. In our denomination, when there is no permanent rector, the senior warden is the responsible person, so my job was interesting. Larry was part of all the meetings at home, at church, or out of town. We did everything together.

Our other career as lifetime medical patients began right after marriage because I wasn't sure I could take care of this man's physical problems. Larry saw many specialists and went to the Mayo Clinic in Rochester to confirm what we all knew about his lung condition. Over the years he had many X-rays, electrocardiograms, CAT scans, bone scans, MRI brain scan, all confirming the fact that he hurt all over. He had bouts with bronchitis and pneumonia, each brought under control with antibiotics.

Then it was my turn. During the first snowfall of the season, I went out to walk in the lovely softness, to feel the icy crystals touch on my face. While rounding the curved road to our house, my foot hit a patch of ice beneath the thin snow, and down I went. I immediately knew that my right wrist was broken, which would involve a one-day stay in the hospital. A neighbor kindly came in to stay with Larry because he would have been upset and disoriented in the house alone. While I recuperated at home, Larry tried to help by washing dishes and waiting on me. Thanks to "Meals on the Go" home deliveries for a couple of weeks, we kept going.

Larry began to fall. The first time it happened, we were in Willmar, where we went to meet his family in a park. He started down the grassy slope to the picnic table and tumbled. His brothers helped him up, but they didn't seem to realize that he had become weaker. Parkinson's disease was beginning to take hold of him, and it caused his feet to lock up sometimes.

The first time he fell in our house, I called the police, thinking they would come and pick him up. They did come, but they brought along the emergency squad and ambulance, and they took him to the hospital for the night. I didn't call them anymore when he fell. If it was obvious there was no injury, I let Larry calm himself and made him comfortable with pillows until he could pull himself up on a chair with my help. It worked.

During a routine visit to the clinic in January 2000, his doctor became excited and immediately started calling to arrange home delivery of oxygen equipment for Larry and a nebulizer for respiratory treatments. He arranged for nurses and social workers to come to our house and evaluate our equipment, accessibility, and my ability to take care of Larry.

The doctor was taking this very seriously, but we were a little amused at all the health professionals swarming through our house, looking at the bathroom, measuring doors and halls, interviewing us, checking out our eating habits, etc. because we had been coping with these details by ourselves for eight years. But they were very helpful, and after a couple of weeks they established a regular routine for monitoring our needs.

In April of 2000, I tripped over Larry's oxygen tubing while hurrying to answer the phone. I heard the crack as I hit the floor and knew there was another broken bone—this time at the top of my left arm. A doctor bound it up tightly in a sling and left it to heal. Poor Larry would snuggle up to me at night, and I would quickly say, "Oh, no, sweetheart, not tonight! I have a broken arm!"

"Oh, honey, I forgot!"

In July Larry spent another week in the hospital, and this time he came home with a wheelchair.

CHAPTER 27

Days Winding Down

As the clear fall days of early October came around, I had a longing to do something exciting just for me, and was able to find a volunteer to stay with Larry for a couple of hours. I hadn't piloted a plane since ten years before when I had a biennial flight review at Crystal Airport in Minneapolis. Now in Albert Lea, I knew a fellow 99s member (International Women Pilots Organization) who was an instructor, and I made an appointment with her for a lesson.

This was very different from my experiences at big city airports. I drove to Marcie's farm west of town and turned onto the long dirt road to the barn. Her older Cessna 172 was sitting outside waiting for me. After pre-flight inspection, I stepped up into the left seat, Marcie took the right seat, and we taxied down a narrow dirt road, across a tiny wooden bridge and into a cornfield. Turning left, we negotiated our way through an area flanked by tall cornstalks before reaching a beautiful, grassy runway, plenty wide enough. I taxied to the west end, made a 180-degree turn, gave her full throttle and took off. Marcie took control because I had no experience on a grass field. Once aloft, I took the controls again and flew over familiar lakes and city parks and neighborhoods. After waving to her husband on his tractor plowing the field, she took over the landing because I could not have found her runway among the miles of green vegetation. It was so exhilarating! I would obviously need to have many more lessons to be able to renew my license, and that was not possible. But what a great way that was to treat myself once in awhile.

In early December, Larry's daughter Molly flew in from southern California to Minneapolis and came down to spend a week with us. It was a difficult trip in cold weather, and she had her first experience with snow. She loved it. We had fun together, and she was so helpful.

As the circling years brought us to January 2001, Larry was again hospitalized for lung infection. His case got a little more complicated when he got up from the bed, forgot that he was attached to several machines, fell and bruised his entire left hip and leg. He remained in the hospital for six days. We had planned to fly to San Diego to escape winter, but we were grounded.

January was the last month of my duties as senior warden for the church. After the annual meeting, when all the new officers were elected, my urge to flee responsibilities and cold weather was so strong that I booked a flight to San Diego for mid-March, when I believed Larry would have regained his strength.

Even though travel had become more complicated, I became pretty good at making necessary arrangements. We would drive to Minneapolis and stay one night at a motel, which allowed us to leave our car in their lot for two weeks if we stayed again on the night of our return. Their shuttle took us to the airport and picked us up when we returned. I ordered oxygen for the night in the motel and arranged for the airline to provide oxygen during our flight. I made the same arrangements for the return flight and time spent at the San Diego airport. Tanks and a concentrator were to be delivered to the house where we would be staying, and Larry's wheelchair was to be put on the plane and ready to use on the Jetway when we deplaned. We would pick up a rental car in San Diego. Each step in this travel plan worked smoothly, and we arrived at my sister's house in Cardiff to enjoy the sun.

CHAPTER 28

A Close Call

Several days after this sunny transition, Larry's health took a turn for the worse. I took him to the emergency room in Cardiff on March 27. I thought they would give him an antibiotic and send him home and he would be noticeably improved in a few days. That's the way it had always worked. But the doctor was very alarmed by his condition and put a tube into his lungs to assist his breathing. He remained in the Intensive Care Unit for quite a few days before they moved him to a private room.

The doctor was urging me to make special plans for Larry because he obviously didn't want to release him. He suggested nursing homes and board and care facilities because he didn't think he could release him to me. Of course, we were strangers to him, and he knew nothing of our lifestyle or of my caregiving capabilities.

Molly came down from Huntington Beach for a couple of days, and we looked at nursing homes. Some were too grand, some were too small, and the whole scene felt surreal. I couldn't picture Larry living with these strangers in a new town. The doctor suggested I leave Larry in a nursing home, fly back to Albert Lea by myself, sell my house and find a place to live in North San Diego County. That would mean packing, hiring a moving van, flying back to California and finding someone willing to bring my car. It would take at least a month, if everything happened smoothly.

Being a responsible, sensible wife, I seriously tried to visualize doing this, accepting the workload, the separation and worry. Every day I would visit Larry hoping to see recovery in his breathing, but days went by until our scheduled departure date had come and gone. I called the airline and received assurance that we could fly on our tickets at a later date, for an extra fee. I was willing to fly home alone, and there was a care facility that was ready to receive Larry. But because of his past life in nursing homes and the improvement he had demonstrated since he started receiving individualized care from me, I didn't want to institutionalize him again, and my frustration grew each day. Finally, his condition began to improve.

"I really want to take Larry back to the house where we are staying," I told his doctor. "I think he will be happier there. This waiting and uncertainty are so hard on us."

It may seem that I was being selfish wanting to take him out of the hospital, with all its equipment and professional nursing care. But experience told me that he was happier at home, near friends. I had seen him rally so many times before, and I knew how to take care of him.

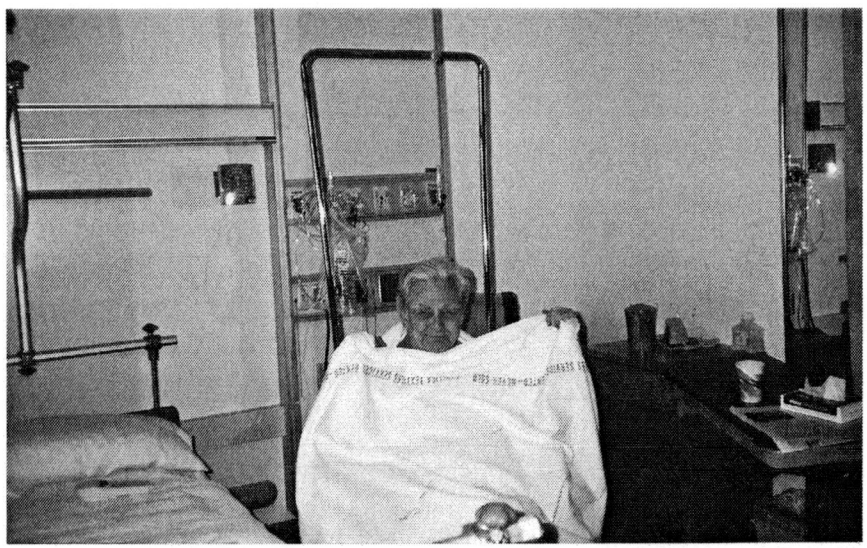

Finally, his condition began to improve.

"Well," the doctor said, "he is strong enough now, but it may not last long. You should go back on the plane as soon as possible."

I had decided the nursing home plan was just unacceptable. He wanted to go home and be left alone to recuperate at his own slow pace.

The next day was Sunday, his thirteenth day in the hospital, and I brought him home to Cardiff. We both relaxed and decided to rest there for five more days. Larry was able to cope with our simple life again.

We made it to the airport with our medical equipment, and in four hours were back in Minneapolis to spend the night in a motel, pick up our car, and drive to Albert Lea.

It was good to be home, but seeds had been planted in my mind to seriously think about moving back to California. In the following weeks, I talked to a realtor about selling our house and began to look on the Internet for a house to buy in North San Diego County.

With the strain of caregiving increasing, I tried taking Larry to day care at Good Samaritan, one of the nursing homes in Albert Lea, where I knew some of the staff. We tried it for a couple of months, but for him it was just warehousing. He would not enter into the life there, and just sat and waited for me to pick him up at the end of each day. Although it gave me a break, it was not the solution for us. We wanted him to have a meaningful, interesting life as a private citizen. That's what we were all about. Somehow we would continue that way.

CHAPTER 29

Go West Old Man!

In June of 2001, I was still driving Larry out to the Good Samaritan nursing home every weekday, and his health was quite stable. Although I knew he would never adapt, he was at least familiar with their routine and personnel.

Marion and her husband were coming to the Kansas City area to perform at a dinner theater for a couple of months. That is an easy drive from Albert Lea, and I wanted to see her. When I found out that a friend of mine would be in Kansas at the same time, that convinced me to go. Since Larry was already oriented to being at "Good Sam," I could arrange for him to stay there for five days so I would be free to travel and enjoy peace of mind about his care.

We had never been completely away from each other since we were married, but this little getaway would provide a good rest and total change for me. I would go first to Atchison, Kansas, Amelia Earhart's birthplace, for their annual Forest of Friendship celebration. This is held in a large park created by the 99s, International Women Pilots, who plant trees to honor people who have made outstanding contributions to the field of aviation. Leah Liersch, my friend from San Diego, was being so honored that summer. What a great opportunity this was to see her and spend two days with women pilots from all over the country. We stayed in the dorms on a small campus and were entertained with tours and banquets.

From Atchison I drove to Overland Park, where I stayed with Larry's brother Gary and his family. On Sunday evening, he and his wife Florence and daughter Dana and I had a wonderful night out at the dinner theater. The food was superb, and the play about an elderly couple was warmly human and funny. After the performance, we joined the cast and management for a quick ride to a sidewalk café in downtown Kansas City. We spent a couple of hours there in boisterous laughter, critiquing the play as the actors unwound from all the excitement. A full moon shone down on the warm summer evening and on horse-drawn carriages that rolled by, outlined with tiny twinkling lights.

I spent the night at Gary's house, and the next morning I drove to Marion's condo. We went back to the same sidewalk café for breakfast. This weekend was another of many impulsive visits with my sister, always short but always energizing events. After breakfast, I said my good byes and headed north to Albert Lea.

Could any travel agent have dreamed up a better four-day vacation? I think not. But I did feel incomplete without Larry. I felt vulnerable without him, like a ship lost at sea. It was a relief to find him okay and ready to return to the safe haven of our home.

Throughout this time, my efforts to move to California were gaining momentum. The thought of going through another cold winter with Larry's health declining confirmed my decision. If we were to make another journey across country, this might be the last time he could stand it. Perhaps a warmer climate might prolong his life a little.

In August, I asked Marion to go with a real estate agent in Encinitas to see some of the houses he suggested. She graciously took the time, and within one morning, she found a great place in Oceanside.

"This is it! This is perfect." She told the realtor. In a quick phone call to me she said, "You have to act fast on this one and make a bid." Emailed pictures of the house and interior convinced me to do as she had advised.

I arranged the loan on the Internet with a company that was already handling some of my financial business, and within a couple of days, emails, faxes and Fed Ex letters were flying back and forth. It was a very smooth and efficient process. I put our Albert Lea home up for sale, signed a contract with a moving company, and set a date for departure. A flurry of packing boxes, garage sales, giving things away, farewell parties and tears began. Larry appeared to be undisturbed by it all. If life became too hectic, he just went to sleep.

Escrow on the new condo in Oceanside was set to close on September 15, 2001, and we made our plans to be there.

CHAPTER 30

Disintegration

What is this force that compels me to move occasionally? This wind at my back energizes me and draws me forward with plans and hopes of fresh new life. My mind is clear, enthusiastic, and capable of stepping up to any challenge with assurance.

In this spirit we began filling boxes, and our friends Gail and Jim came to help pack. On Monday morning, September 10, two men from the moving company worked steadily, packing large cartons. Both our televisions were boxed and taped up, along with almost everything else, and the movers left us just enough stuff to get by for two more nights.

The next morning, September 11, I gathered up my last remaining belongings while listening to the radio, which had escaped being packed because it was still screwed to the kitchen cupboard. The usual morning chatter was interrupted by a news bulletin.

"Larry, listen ... there seems to be something serious happening in New York. Something has hit a big building ... the World Trade Center ...what is that? Oh my God, they say an airplane hit it! And it's collapsing! How horrible!"

Larry didn't seem to grasp the reality of this news, and it was only dimly forming in my consciousness. We continued working in our own small world while the radio unfolded this growing calamity throughout the day. We were spared the full impact because our televisions were packed away, and we couldn't see any of the news pictures.

The next day we continued packing, and on Thursday, September 13, the huge van arrived. Men emptied our house, packed the van from floor to ceiling, and left at noon for California. Several days on the road was out of the question for Larry, so Gail and Jim agreed to drive us to Minneapolis. After having dinner with us, they left us at our motel and started their long drive to San Diego in our car. What good friends they were! We hoped it would be a fun vacation for them, at least.

The motel lobby was crowded with people who had been waiting days to get on their planes, and two days post 911, not many flights had been resumed. We heard warnings about delays but decided to be ready to leave as planned the next morning. The shuttle took us to the airport, with the oxygen tank and wheelchair.

After going through security checks and arriving at our gate, we were told that our flight had been canceled, but the airline hoped to have another flight available about 6:30 in the evening. Airline staff were very attentive and took us to the Traveler's Aid private lounge, where we were allowed to stay all day. The room was furnished with soft recliner chairs. Several large TVs gave us our first view of the disastrous attack on the World Trade Center and Pentagon. We could watch only so long, and then we would go out to escape the intensity, and I would push Larry's wheelchair down almost-empty halls. Airport employees, maintenance people and vendors opened their stalls, but the place was eerily quiet, with just a few people moving slowly and talking in hushed tones. We stopped at a nice restaurant for a hamburger lunch. Larry was having difficulty eating his sandwich and was becoming irritable so I asked the waiter for a knife to cut the burger in half.

"I'm sorry, Ma'am, there are no knives allowed in the airport, for security reasons."

"Not even plastic knives?" I asked.

"No, I'm sorry."

"Well, could you take it to the kitchen and have someone split it?" He agreed to that, and we finally ate our lunch, which had lost some of its appeal.

We found a beauty shop next to the lounge, and since we had so much time, we both had our hair cut. Larry had a manicure, and he enjoyed all the special attention and the chance to flirt a little. It was an expensive pastime.

Late in the afternoon, the loudspeaker announced that our flight was canceled because they could not get a crew. Fortunately, we were able to secure a room back at the motel for another night, and the next morning we departed at the scheduled time.

The flight was easy. As I was leaving the plane in San Diego, I looked for someone from the oxygen company to be there with a tank, but there was no one. I had overlooked calling to tell them we would arrive a day late. It was Saturday, and their office was closed. The flight attendant saw our problem and let us have a tank from the aircraft's supply, only for use while in the airport. While pushing Larry's wheelchair down to the baggage carousels, I realized that the oxygen was not turned on, even though the hose was attached. After trying and failing to find the valve, I got help from Travelers Aid to call the after-hours number of the supplier, who had probably shown up at the airport the day before. Larry was not complaining, but he was beginning to look gray. Airport paramedics were called, and three of them studied the equipment, baffled. Finally, one reached up inside the wooden box that enclosed the tank and found the valve hidden from sight.

Three hours after we landed, a driver arrived with a tank for us to take home and arranged to meet us at the house in Cardiff with an oxygen concentrator. We picked up the rental car and finally arrived at our house by suppertime.

Two days later, Gail and Jim arrived with our car. They stayed four days, and helped us move into our new condo in Oceanside when the van arrived. Living in California meant that I was closer to my sons and their wives, my grandchildren and my sister, and that felt good. We settled in, and suffered no ill effects from that somewhat hectic trip. But like everyone else in America, we would not soon forget that week in September.

In California with Joel's children, David and Elizabeth

CHAPTER 31

In Sickness and Health

"Isn't it great to have no steps to climb, no snow to shovel and no ice to fall on!" Larry agreed with me; he always liked California.

We cheerfully settled into the new condo high on a hilltop in Oceanside, where fresh sea breezes swept through our windows. In this quiet, neat, senior community we made new friends and kept busy re-establishing our routines. I found new doctors and contacted North County Council on Aging to help find home health aides for weekly visits. I spent much time making myself known to California's notorious DMV while trying to become a bona fide resident and licensed driver.

Larry seemed contented. He was more cautious about walking and did not fall down. Using the wheelchair, we went to the mall shopping, to picnics in the parks, the beach, and even took a drive north of Los Angeles for Thanksgiving. After Christmas, my son Pat and his family came down for a quick visit. My grandson Everett was to be honored at his Eagle Scout Award program in Temecula with all his family and friends in attendance, and we were happy to be there.

Larry's daughter Molly was able to come to our home for overnight visits. Life was filling up with the good times with family and friends we had hoped for. We even went to the Olive Garden for lunch one day in January and shared some wine while we relaxed.

Larry with Molly, her husband Tom, and Ruie

"Now this is the way I used to live!" Larry announced with a smile of approval. We forgot about the inconvenience of his weakened physical condition and enjoyed the ambience of old Italy.

One morning a few weeks later, Larry discovered a growth in his nostril, a polyp. It was hanging out of his nose and looked so bizarre. Neither of us had ever seen anything like it. We went to a nose and throat specialist who assured us it was common and could be removed by a simple operation at the clinic where his office was located near Scripps Hospital in Encinitas. We set up an appointment for February 5, and we waited patiently for the day, trying not to worry.

When the day came, we checked into the waiting room, and by mid-afternoon Larry was taken into the operating area while I waited in the office. The doctor had told me that the anesthesiologist had opted to use a general anesthetic rather than the usual local. They were afraid of Larry's mental disability and thought he might react forcibly to having them work so close to his face. It sounded logical, and I agreed with them.

I waited over an hour, and by then I was the only person left in the waiting room. Winter days are short, and it was getting dark, almost quitting time for the staff. I decided to use the restroom and went out into the hall to find it. I returned to the waiting room, and to my dismay, found the door locked. Lights were turned off in the office, and no one was in the entry hall. Looking about in perplexity, I spotted a telephone that was labeled "for use of family of patients in the operating room." I tried dialing the number shown, but there was no answer. Where was Larry? A man came into the hall and opened one of several doors. After he came out again, I tried the same door.

I found myself in a long, narrow space that looked like an emergency room, but it was dark except for a lighted area at the far end where the nurses were. One of them came to tell me that I shouldn't be there, but since there was no other available place for me to be, she let me stay. She said that Larry had not come out of the anesthetic as expected, and they were trying to revive him and give him oxygen.

They would have to send him across the parking lots to Scripps Emergency Room. They had called the ambulance, and paramedics were talking to nurses in urgent tones. It sounded to me as if they were questioning their authorization or responsibility to take Larry on this short ride. Time seemed to stand still as I sat in the dark listening to their mumbled argument around Larry's gurney. I was praying so hard that this impasse would be broken. Finally, I could no longer be passive, and walked up to the group. My presence seemed to motivate a response, and there was now movement as they began to load the stretcher.

I said as I pushed towards him, "I have to let him know I am here. He can't hear you without his hearing aids. He doesn't know what is happening."

His eyes met mine as they rolled him onto the ambulance. "Honey, I'm coming with you, right behind you. You'll be all right. I love you!"

I hopped into my car and followed the ambulance to Scripps ER, where medical professionals spent the evening settling Larry into a life support system in the Intensive Care Unit. What had begun that morning as a simple procedure had become another detour to the edge of eternity.

CHAPTER 32

The Comeback Kid

"I don't understand; he didn't seem that sick when he was in my office," said the nasal specialist as he was walking out of Larry's room in Intensive Care. "The surgery was successful and seemed routine so I left immediately after we were finished. He seemed to be strong."

"Yes, he is a fighter. He is unpredictable. One day he can feel miserable, and the next day he is jovial and energetic. Anxiety and breathing difficulty sap his strength."

"Well, I will look in on him for the next couple of days. Good luck," said the doctor as he walked away, and I entered the Intensive Care Ward. I was determined to be with Larry every day for as long as possible and would not allow anyone to put me out of his room. The nurses soon understood that I would not get in their way and that I could help them understand him better. I vowed to be more assertive this time. Since he had tubes in his mouth to assist his breathing, and he was heavily sedated, as well as deaf, I thought he needed an interpreter.

Larry remained on life support for a few days. I spent the first night at Marion's house in Cardiff just a mile away, but most nights I drove home to Oceanside, about seventeen miles. One morning, I happily learned that his breathing had improved, and the tube had been removed. He seemed to be doing better until afternoon, when the doctor came and spoke to me.

"Your husband isn't going to make it on his own. His oxygen level is falling. He needs to be intubated again to survive.

Do you want him to go through this again? It's up to you. We need to have your decision right now."

I felt anger rising in me. I felt trapped. Perhaps I should have been ready long ago for such a question, but how does one prepare to make instant, unstudied decisions that will end or prolong another person's life? The doctor seemed angry too; he had been working very hard to save Larry.

Yielding to pressure, finally I said, "All right! All right! Do it this one more time, but after that, no more!" I left the room this time while they did their work. Was I just being selfish putting Larry through this ordeal again? I wasn't ready to lose him that night; it seemed inconceivable. There wasn't anyone present to advise me, and there wasn't time to call anyone for support. I drove home.

Fortunately, the next day he began to improve and was breathing on his own again by late in the day. He was gradually moved into more regular hospital rooms. After fourteen days of hospitalization, he was transferred to a nursing home on February 18. He had only been there for six hours when I received a phone call informing me they did not have the equipment to treat his breathing problems, and they were sending him back to Scripps Hospital. When would this end? He couldn't go on living in a hospital!

Four days later, the doctor told me there was no more that he could do for Larry and he was transferring him to a hospice program. Larry came home in an ambulance on Friday, February 22, and I was grateful to have him back in our own little abode, as he always called it. We could face anything when we had each other and our faith in the Holy Trinity, another of his favorite expressions.

A hospital bed was set up in the living room by the picture window, where Larry could look out across the canyon.

A team of nurses and a male aide set up a schedule of weekly visits to take care of bathing and monitoring his medications. New medications were delivered to the house. The hospice staff was very helpful, both physically and psychologically. They deal with this type of situation on a daily basis so they know what to do.

Larry became steadily stronger. He was soon able to sit in his wheelchair and have his meals at the dining table. His hair had turned white, but his disposition was quite good. We returned to normal living patterns more and more each week. His brother Neal and his wife Jan came to visit, and his sister Ruie Helen and her husband Tom spent a couple of days with us. His daughter Molly came too. It was a precious time.

March 2001

CHAPTER 33

The Final Journey

Grateful to be home together again, we adapted our schedule to the visits of the hospice nurses. Dwayne, the personal care aide, and Jackie, the nurse, came twice a week. The social worker came occasionally to inquire about my needs. Messengers came promptly whenever we needed prescription refills. They were all very kind, but Larry didn't warm up to any of them, which was atypical of his usual gregarious personality. He must have realized that this was serious business, even though I didn't discuss the significance of being cared for by hospice or that his days were numbered.

On Sundays a couple from Saint Anne's Episcopal Church, Angie and Kirk, came to bring us the reserved sacrament of communion. They usually stayed about an hour and became dear friends. We found a barber, Johnny, who came to give Larry a haircut and chat a bit.

Larry's need for special nursing diminished, and we asked to have the hospital bed put into the spare bedroom. He tried sleeping in our own bed, which was comforting to both of us. We had the other bed as a backup when he was too restless. He still needed oxygen day and night and breathing treatments throughout the day.

One of the benefits that hospice offered was respite care for five days so that I could have some time off. I decided to take advantage of that and booked Larry into a nearby nursing home. It took most of a day to get him settled into new quarters. I had called a pilot friend, Gus, and hired him to fly me to Imperial out in the desert so I could visit my youngest son. It had been years since I had seen him. Gus was happy to oblige and didn't mind waiting for me while I visited Daniel. And I enjoyed flying in a small plane again, even if it was in the right seat!

Larry seemed to be all right when I picked him up couple of days later. With me pushing his wheelchair down the block, he was able to attend the July 4th party at our clubhouse to celebrate his 77th birthday.

Days flowed peacefully into summer, and we spent hours on the patio enjoying the breezes and chatting with neighbors. We didn't go on outings anymore because his breathing was more difficult and there was much congestion in his lungs. Sometimes he would smile at me across the room and his lips would form the words, "I love you," but no sound would come out. I thought it was sweet, and my mind refused to grasp the reason he was silent.

My daughter-in-law Karen came down from northern California to pick up Everett, her son, from San Pedro. He was beaming with excitement when they came to tell us about his summer at Boy Scout Camp on Catalina Island. Karen was staying nearby in Escondido with her mother for a couple of weeks and we enjoyed having them over for several visits.

One Thursday morning in late July, Dwayne came to get Larry bathed and dressed. I had fixed a good breakfast of waffles for Larry. Karen arrived, and she and I went out for coffee in a restaurant, a good chance to relax for a couple of hours and catch up on family news. We were light hearted and chatty like a couple of schoolgirls.

When we returned at noon, Jackie was there. Larry was slumped in his wheelchair dozing, his waffles cut neatly but untouched. Jackie said he hadn't been doing so well that morning. I asked if they could send out some antibiotic, which usually helped when he was so congested. She and Dwayne left, and then Karen left to go to her mother's house, so we were alone. Larry was too sleepy to eat lunch so I wheeled him into the bedroom to help him get into the hospital bed. He stood up but was so weak I had to actually lift some of his weight, for the first time. He slept, and late in the afternoon he was awake enough to take some medicine, but not enough to eat dinner.

The next morning, I was not able to wake him. I called our friend Kirk and asked, "Would you pray for Larry? He doesn't seem to be doing well today."

"Certainly. I'll tell Angie, and we'll both pray for him. God bless you both." Kirk responded immediately.

I called Jackie to ask if she could come and check on Larry. "I'm with another patient right now, but I will come as soon as possible. Are you all right?" she asked. I believe that she knew, based on her significant experience and his recent decline, that his death was imminent.

"I'm okay," I replied with the assurance that comes from numbness.

Each time I went into the bedroom to check on him, Larry's color was changing. I had seen it go from dark gray to pale to soft alabaster. I knew he was leaving this world, and I sadly accepted this reality because I knew he was ready.

The doorbell rang, and I was relieved to think that Jackie had come. But instead, it was the large figure of Father Tony, our priest, who stood in the doorway. Kirk must have called him. He walked in immediately to Larry's bedside and said the prayers commending his soul to Almighty God while I stood by Larry's side and joined in the prayers.

Jackie came soon after that and took charge, knowing everything that needed to be done.

Being surrounded by such caring and competent people, I relaxed. Father Tony graciously listened while I released my emotional story and its complex contours that I had kept to myself for so many years–the highs and lows, the disappointment and the joy, of this remarkable sixty-seven-year relationship. Telling my story gave me a feeling of relief rather than sadness. Father Tony made arrangements to accompany me to the mortuary later that afternoon. I will forever be grateful to him for his comforting support.

I flew back to Minnesota, where Larry's funeral was held July 31 at St. Luke's Episcopal Church in Willmar, the church where he and his ten siblings grew up and where he had been an acolyte as a young boy. Our friend Father Jim Jenkins came from Minneapolis to officiate, and a group of friends from our church in Albert Lea were kind enough to make the long drive.

Larry was laid to rest with military honors beside the graves of his mother, father and baby sister. With his brothers and sisters and many other relatives gathered around, he was gently settled in the ground beneath the sheltering branches of great oak trees by the side of a lake. The service was a dignified end to his difficult mortal life.

As we left the church, one of Larry's boyhood friends came up and shook my hand. It was Dick Hoagland, former mayor of Willmar. "You know," he said, "Larry and I spent many hours together playing at his house and in the neighborhood when we were just kids. He used to say, 'When I grow up, I am going to marry Alicia Ross!' "

Who would think that such a few words could fill my heart with joy? I knew in my heart that my decision to reunite with the love of my life was a wise and wonderful thing to do. I did not need to hear affirmation that it had been right to follow my heart and take a huge leap of faith that required me to accept the past and embrace the joys and realities of the present. But Dick Hoagland's words showed that others understood, and that meant the world to me. "Oh, you have given me a great gift. Thank you so much."

Back home in Oceanside, my days alone were strange but not oppressive. In a dream one early morning, I looked out the dining room window and saw Larry tall, straight, and slim as in his youth. He was standing some distance away, suspended above the canyon in the back yard. He was waving at me. I knew it was Larry, and I knew I must wave back. While struggling to lift my sleep-deadened arm, I woke to find that arm flailing back and forth. I had answered him. Now I knew he was not really gone; he was just on the other side of the window, waiting for me.

Q & A With the Author

Q. Your story ends in 2002. What are you doing today?

A. Ten years after Larry's death, I am once again living in southern Minnesota. I fill my time by getting out into my community, chatting with people and making new friends. I am still an active member of the Episcopal Church, where I serve on the Vestry, which is the governing board. I'm really too old to take on such a big responsibility, but they need the help and I enjoy spending time with these people, some of whom I've known since childhood. I believe that a good, solid Christian way of life is healthy for both the individual and the community.

Once a week I volunteer at the local historical society, helping to organize files and identify photographs, and pitching in whenever they have special events and projects. They are currently expanding their museum, which is an exciting thing to watch. I attend concerts, plays and art shows in my little city, and sometimes I just get out and walk. After many years, I gave up playing piano and gave my Solmar grand to the church, where it can be enjoyed by many for years to come.

I usually spend some of the winter months with my sons in California. And just a few days before this book went to print, I drove with a small group to Kansas City and visited Marion, who was starring in a production of *The Game's Afoot* at the New Theatre.

Q. What are your thoughts on computers, technology and the younger generation?

A. I try to keep up with computers and technology, but I constantly observe that the space between me and the younger generation gets wider daily, but not any less enjoyable. I hold out great hope for the young. There is no telling what they will invent. History will look upon them as the group that changed things the most.

Q. Writing this book after so many years must have dredged up a variety of emotions. Did you find that difficult?

A. I really enjoyed working on this project because I began feeling closer to Larry as a real person, and it was almost therapeutic. I can see that this is not some vaporous dream that I had, but an amazing experience, a significant part of my life spent with a man I really loved.

Q. Do you have any life lessons you'd be willing to share?

A. Every day I learn new things, but here are four somewhat profound lessons I don't mind sharing:

• I've learned not to be angry at people, because it's hard on me and they have problems of their own.

• My own path has had moments of success as well as failure, all of them stepping stones to a more fulfilling life.

• I've learned to keep my mouth shut and try to weigh a situation before speaking out. You have to consider so many things before you react.

• Instead of being angry and wanting to dismiss a person who caused a problem, turning around and doing a kind act can turn a negative situation to a positive one. Instead of blowing your top when someone has terribly upset or agitated you, go the opposite direction and react with love. A little patience, some dialogue and a willingness to listen thoughtfully before reacting can produce a much better result. Thousands of people must have said this before!

Q. Do you still fly that little Cessna?

A. I no longer pilot a plane, but I believe that many lessons learned in the air are applicable on the ground. Flying a plane requires meticulous adherence to details. You learn your procedures and proper sequences. Before your trip, you learn what hazards you might expect to meet, then study your route until you know it by heart so that you can react to unexpected developments calmly and reasonably. You know what your plane is physically capable of doing, and you observe the weather at your point of departure, at each point along your route, and at your destination. You know your own abilities and whether or not you can handle the situation, always keeping in mind your physical and psychological condition.

An instructor or a good pilot will say, "If the winds are too unpredictable or if the cloud ceiling is too low, you might have to delay the flight."